C000165922

An Introduction to the Philosophy of Mind

An Introduction to the Philosophy of Mind

David Cockburn
Professor of Philosophy
University of Wales, Lampeter

For Sean and Patrick

First published 2001 by
PALGRAVE
Houndmills, Basingstoke, Hampshire RG21 6XS and
175 Fifth Avenue, New York, N. Y. 10010
Companies and representatives throughout the world

PALGRAVE is the new global academic imprint of
St. Martin's Press LLC Scholarly and Reference Division and
Palgrave Publishers Ltd (formerly Macmillan Press Ltd).

ISBN 0–333–78637–8 hardback
ISBN 0–333–96122–6 paperback

This book is printed on paper suitable for recycling and
made from fully managed and sustained forest sources.

A catalogue record for this book is available
from the British Library.

Library of Congress Cataloging-in-Publication Data
Cockburn, David, 1949–
    An introduction to the philosophy of mind / David Cockburn.
      p. cm.
    Includes bibliographical references (p.) and index.
    ISBN 0–333–78637–8 (cloth) — ISBN 0–333–96122–6 (pbk.)
    1. Philosophy of mind. I. Title.

    BD418.3 .C59 2001
    128'.2—dc21

                   00–054531

10 9 8 7 6 5 4 3 2 1
10 09 08 07 06 05 04 03 02 01

Printed and bound in Great Britain by
Antony Rowe Ltd, Chippenham, Wiltshire

Contents

Acknowledgements

Some of the material in Chapter 3 originally appeared in *Philosophy*. Chapter 9 is a revised and expanded version of an article that was published in *Cogito*. I am grateful to the editors of these journals for permission to use this material here.

Preface

The aims of a book title are, I guess, to catch the potential reader's attention and to give him or her some idea of what the book is about. I will use this Preface to provide a long footnote (the only footnote in the book I should perhaps hasten to add!) to my title.

This book has, roughly speaking, the form of a debate between three broad approaches to the question 'What is a person?' The three terms in the main sub-title – 'souls', 'science' and 'human beings' – are an attempt to pin brief, and memorable, labels on these approaches. Central to the first view is the idea that what I essentially am is a non-material entity – a 'mind' or 'soul' – which, while it in some sense inhabits this body for the period of my life as a human being, is quite distinct from it. This is often regarded as a traditional view of the person: and one that has been largely discredited by advances in the physical sciences. The second of my three approaches presents matters in this way, suggesting that it is to such sciences that we must look if we are to attain a proper understanding of what a person is: the description of a person, and the explanations of her behaviour, that are offered by physical science are the fundamental truth about what she is. While in one of its forms this approach suggests that the mind is the brain and that mental states are states of the brain, that familiar thought has, over the past thirty years, been modified in response to various objections. According to the third of the three approaches, to attain philosophical clarity we must give a fundamental place to the idea that the person is the human being – the bodily being that we encounter in our everyday interactions with others – and to the ways in which we respond to each other in such interactions.

While I have done my best to present the arguments for each of these approaches as fairly as possible I have made no attempt to disguise my own position. The perceptive reader might already have a pretty shrewd idea of where I stand. In any case, I must now comment on the main title in terms that will let the cat decisively out of the bag.

It is with considerable misgivings that I have described this book as 'An Introduction to the Philosophy of Mind'. While I hope that this will help to give the potential reader an indication of what is to be found in the book, it may, for all that, be seriously misleading in various respects. First, a bookshop browser might expect such a book to

convey a good picture of what the largest number of cleverest philosophers have been saying about 'the mind' over the last twenty or thirty
years. But, while two chapters of this book are devoted to an attempt
to do something like that, the book as a whole has a different aim. For
I am inclined to think that what the largest number of cleverest
philosophers have being saying about 'the mind' over the last twenty
or thirty years – while it includes material of great importance –
bypasses many of the issues that have been central to traditional philosophical thought about human beings and their place in the world;
and with that, bypasses a range of issues that might be of concern to a
reflective person who looks to philosophy for some insight in this area.

A second respect in which the title may be misleading is this. A
potential reader might reasonably expect that this book will be about
'the mind'. But the book is not about 'the mind'. It is about people:
human beings. And one of the central contentions of the book might
be formulated in this way: it is extremely unhelpful to articulate what
distinguishes a person from an inanimate object by saying that the former, but not the latter, 'has a mind'. That is not to deny that people –
and, indeed, some non-human creatures – have minds. It is simply to
say that the idea that 'the mind' is the place where all the most distinctively human activities – thought, emotion, sensation and so on –
occur sets the whole discussion off on quite the wrong foot. René
Descartes (1596–1650) is widely credited with the main responsibility
for having set modern Western philosophy on this path. But, however
that may be, I believe that much philosophical thinking still reflects
the stranglehold of this disastrous imagery; and I would hate to think
that my use of the conventional phrase – 'the philosophy of mind' –
might do anything to reinforce that hold.

Perhaps there is a third respect in which the title could be misleading. There is rather more talk of relationships between people, and of
the ways in which people *matter* to us, than some might have expected
in a book on 'the philosophy of mind'. This stands in contrast to a certain picture of the character of philosophy: a picture that would imply
that an investigation of what a person *is* is quite distinct from, and perhaps prior to, any investigation of a broadly 'ethical' form. The discussion of this book, however, rests on – and I hope to some extent
vindicates – the assumption that this picture is not a helpful one. For I
believe that one of the things that is distinctive of a philosophical
understanding in this, and other, areas is the way in which these forms
of inquiry are brought together.

My treatment of the topics discussed draws heavily on the work of a man whom many consider to be the greatest philosopher of the twentieth century: Ludwig Wittgenstein (1889–1951). While at a number of points I explicitly attempt to present some of his ideas, this book is not an introduction to Wittgenstein's philosophy. There already exist a number of excellent books of this kind. My aim has been, rather, to produce a text that will introduce the reader to a range of central issues in 'the philosophy of mind' in a way that reflects both the place that these issues have occupied in Modern Philosophy – the European and (more centrally) the English-speaking tradition in philosophy since the time of Descartes – and the transforming insights of Wittgenstein's later thought.

I hope that this book will be accessible to people with little formal background in philosophy, and that it will convey to such a reader a sense of the *importance* of the issues discussed. I am acutely aware, however, that some sections are tougher going than others. The presentation of Wittgenstein's 'private language argument' in sections 3 and 4 of Chapter 4, while I hope being simpler than standard presentations, may call for a kind of mental agility that, perhaps, generally comes only with a substantial period of immersion in certain philosophical ways of thinking. The beginner could, I think, omit these sections without significant impact on his or her understanding of later chapters. (It is possible that the force of the argument in these sections will be more readily apparent after reading section 2 of Chapter 8.) Chapters 5 and 6, in which I present and discuss central aspects of views that have dominated the philosophy of mind for the past forty years or so, also contain material that may be found rather more difficult than the remainder of the book. Those chapters could also be omitted on a first reading without, I think, any noticeable disruption in the flow of the discussion.

The beginner might, I think, be strongly advised to make extensive use of the Analytical Table of Contents. The summary of each chapter might be read both before and after the chapter itself. For purposes of general orientation at particular stages of the book the reader might, periodically, find it useful to read right through the summary up to the point that has been reached.

I have taught courses on the philosophy of mind, and on Wittgenstein, at the University of Wales, Lampeter for the past twenty years. I have benefited from, and enjoyed, these courses enormously. Almost all of the students who have attended those courses have contributed in some way to this book, and I would like to thank them for their enthusiasm, stimulation and insights. I have also benefited from comments on various sections of this book by Ossie Hanfling, Maureen Meehan, April Norden and Bob Sharpe. I would particularly like to thank Andrew Gleeson, who gave me an enormously helpful, and encouraging, set of comments on the whole manuscript at an important stage.

Analytical Table of Contents

the world and the position where that person is. It might be argued that only a Cartesian account – in terms of the idea that the non-material mind left the body – could explain the experiences had; but the Cartesian 'explanation' has gaps of just the same form as alternative explanations.

3. A tension in our thought: We are only inclined to think it is obvious that a person must be located at the point from which she perceives the world because we tacitly assume that people are *human beings* – an assumption on which the dualist can hardly depend.

4. Value, science, and the immaterial: The pull of the Cartesian view is in part dependent on a linking of the 'immaterial' with the idea of 'spiritual' value. But that linking needs defence. The supernaturalist's response to the idea that modern 'natural' science gives us 'the fundamental truth about how things are' reflects a limited under-standing of the *kind* of gap that an account may contain. Various con-trasts – in particular, the 'material'/'immaterial' and 'mind'/'body' contrasts – stand in the way of an acknowledgement that value is to be found in the world of extended, tangible, observable beings.

3   Other Minds

1. The need for justification: Mill suggests that it is similarities in the bodies and behaviour of myself and others that justify my convic-tion that some of those I see around me are beings with feelings like mine. We will think that we need such a justification if we accept Descartes' conception of the self; but we might, independently of that, feel a need for it if confronted with, for example, doubts about the feelings of other species.

2. *Which* bodily similarities are relevant?: In the absence of a demon-stration of *which* bodily similarities and differences are relevant the argument cannot justify what it attempts to. Our instinctive views about which are relevant are *dependent* on our convictions about which creatures have particular feelings.

3. Facial expression and movements of facial flesh: We can distinguish two different *kinds* of 'similarity in behaviour'; for example, there is the similarity between two facial *expressions* and that between two physical arrangements of facial flesh. Once these are distinguished it is not clear that either will serve for Mill's justification.

4. Conclusion: justification and the mind/body divide: The idea that we *need* the argument from analogy depends on an assumption that undermines that argument.

4   Mind and Behaviour

1. Cartesianism and contemporary views: Most contemporary views hold that a person is an extended, tangible being that exists in the same world as that of tables and trees. But this formulation conceals important differences, which reflect different emphases in their criticism of Cartesianism.
2. The social character of our mental vocabulary: A word such as 'anger' is a word in a language that I share with others. If we take this, not the solitary Cartesian individual, as our starting point we will acknowledge that there is a close link between our talk of mental states and the patterns of behaviour in which particular mental states are characteristically expressed.
3. Private language (i): One of the central attractions of the Cartesian approach lies in the idea that I cannot be mistaken in my judgements about my own mental states. But Wittgenstein shows that what is true in that idea is *not* captured in the Cartesian picture.
4. Private language (ii): The idea that 'A person cannot be mistaken about whether or not he is in pain' has the sense that it does, and only *could* have sense, within the context of the close link, stressed by Wittgenstein, between pain and its public expression in behaviour.
5. Knowledge of others: When we understand the relation between mental states and behaviour in the way suggested we see that the difficulties that may be involved in getting to know another are quite different from those suggested by the Cartesian account.
6. The joy in another's face: We have the idea that what we really *see* of another is simply matter in motion; that a strict description of what is seen – say in another's face – will involve no reference to mentality. But there seems to be no reason to accept this. The *philosophical* contrast between 'mental states' and 'behaviour', which implies that all judgements about the former are the result of an inference, is not one that we have to accept.

5   The Material Mind

1. The mind–brain identity thesis: It is widely supposed that contemporary science suggests that one of the steps in Descartes' story – that which involves the non-material 'soul or mind' – is a myth. Some conclude that sensations and so on are not states of (affections of) a non-material mind, but, rather, states of the brain. But it is not clear what evidence would support such a claim.

xiv   *Analytical Table of Contents*

exactly alike in all physical respects cannot differ in mental respects'. A dualist could hold this doctrine, avoiding Descartes' problem by insisting that, while the physical has effects on the mental, the mental has no effects on the physical. But this is an uncomfortable conclusion.

4. Mind–body supervenience – physicalism: A different model of mind–body supervenience might be based on an analogy with the relation between a painting and the patches of paint of which it is composed, or a body of water and the atoms of which it is composed. We might then hold that a mental state is 'nothing over and above' its physical basis, and so perhaps avoid the problems about how the mental can have effects in the physical world.

5. Two doubts about supervenience physicalism: (i) It has been argued that a person's mental states are not supervenient on her physical states since, for example, what thoughts can be ascribed to a person depends, in part, on context; (ii) Even if we could accept the supervenience claim, would it follow that mental states are 'nothing over and above' their physical bases?

6. The attractions of 'physicalism': It is important to remember that the world as presented by contemporary physics is very different from the mechanistic world-view of seventeenth-century physics. Three points that may help to ease the pull of physicalism: (i) The 'problem' that this version of physicalism is trying to resolve may arise from a conflation of the idea that everything that happens in the physical world has entirely physical causes with the idea that nothing that happens in the physical world involves a violation of the laws of physics; (ii) The idea that the 'fundamental causal work' goes on at the level of the elementary particles of which the physicists speak may reflect the outdated metaphysics of seventeenth-century physics; (iii) The idea that everything that happens in the physical world is fixed by what goes on in the micro-world may confront a problem in the question: does the spatial arrangement of the atoms of which a body is composed constitute a 'feature of the micro-world'? The fundamental issue may be not so much whether 'physicalism is true or false', as one of whether the language of physicalism is helpful and illuminating.

7 Human Beings

1. The mind, the body and the human being: Some forms of materialism may share important assumptions with Cartesian dualism.

For example, they may share the assumption that the human body is a 'physical object'. But the terms in which we normally understand human behaviour are not those of the natural sciences. There is a sense in which materialism may simply take over the highly questionable mind/body distinction that is central to dualism; so overlooking the possibility that it is the *human being*, not some part of her, that is in pain or angry.

2. 'An attitude towards a soul': The attraction of dualism may spring in part from the idea that the distinctive range of attitudes that we have towards other people is only in place if a person is something over and above the extended human being. Wittgenstein insists that these attitudes do not require the underpinning of some *belief* that I have about others: they are what is most basic in my relation to the other.

3. The object of pity: The language in which we describe the behaviour of others is a reflection of the ways in which we respond to others; and so it is quite unclear what is the force of the claim, shared by dualist and materialist, that what I actually *see* when I am confronted with another human being is a physical object, no different in kind from any other. Wittgenstein argues not simply that a living human being, and what resembles one, is a possible candidate for the distinctive range of responses to others, but that it is the *only* possible candidate.

4. 'Souls', human beings and animals: For the dualist, one either has a 'mind'/'soul' or one doesn't; and so there is a tendency to flatten out crucial differences in our attitudes towards other creatures. Wittgenstein's approach makes it easier to acknowledge the *particular* range of responses that we owe to particular species.

5. Could a machine think?: In certain discussions of this question we see an appeal to a radical 'mind'/'body' contrast. We see this in the assumptions that are made – for example, in the Turing test – about the kinds of behaviour that might be relevant to the judgement that something thinks; and, linked with that, in the assumption that it is, not human beings, but their *brains* that think.

8 The Identity of the Self

1. Thoughts and thinkers: Does Descartes have grounds for concluding from the fact that there are thoughts that there is a self that has the thoughts?

2. Judging who is in pain: The fact that I do not have to recognize a particular person by his bodily characteristics in order to judge that it is me that is in pain may lead us to think that the real me is a non-bodily being. We see the mistake in this line of argument when we appreciate that, in this case, it does not *make sense* to suppose that I should misidentify who is in pain.

3. Identity and memory: Locke argues that there is a crucial distinction between the 'identity of man' and '*personal* identity'. He also argues, however, that what is crucial to being the same person over time is not 'having the same Cartesian soul', but having an inside awareness – memories – of that person's life. But the apparent attractions of this suggestion depend on an ambiguity in the notion of 'memory'; and Locke's view will have practical consequences that we may be reluctant to accept.

4. 'No-self': Others have argued that there is no more to my being 'the same person' from one day to the next than the holding of certain psychological links between a person on one day and a person on another. But there is disagreement about whether this, if true, would show that there is no important sense in which each of us is the *same* person from one day to another.

5. Personal identity and personal relations: If we take as our starting point our ethical intuitions about cases in which someone for whom we care undergoes radical psychological change we may be more inclined to conclude that 'being the same human being' – the same bodily being – is more central to the idea of being the same person than many philosophers have assumed.

9   Freedom and Science

1. Introduction: Tempting views about a case in which someone's actions are dependent on his having been exposed to brain affecting fumes may imply that science could show that none of us is responsible for anything that we do.

2. Causes and enabling conditions: It seems that, in such cases, it is crucial to ask whether the fumes caused his behaviour or simply *enabled* him to act as he did. But how is that question to be answered?

3. Freedom, science and morality: It may be that what is needed to answer such questions is more akin to ethical thought than to scientific evidence. The question 'Did the chemical cause the behaviour or did it simply enable the man's true self to come out?' may pretty

well just be the, essentially ethical, question 'Is the man to be blamed and punished for what he did?' It may, then, be seriously misleading to suggest that science might establish that all human behaviour is causally determined and so that no one is ever rightly held responsible for anything that they do.

4. 'Could have done otherwise': Might not science show us that nobody could ever act other than they do? Even if it did it would not follow – as we might suppose – that nobody is responsible for what they do. What is crucial is the idea of acting for one's own reasons.

5. Responsibility and the person: Certain considerations suggest that it is not, as such, *determinism* that creates a difficulty for the idea of responsibility. It is more that, when our attention is focused on the micro-world of physiology, we can find no place for the person who is to be held responsible. We find this only when we move back to the level of the human being.

10   Postscript: the Self and the World

1. Souls, brains and human beings: Traditional dualism and certain forms of materialism share the idea of a 'mind' – the part of us that thinks – that is distinct from the bodily human being. This idea may be reflected in our understanding of what we are doing when we are engaged in philosophy.

2. Descartes and 'the external world': Descartes' picture of what he is may precede his conception of what he can doubt; for he assumes that we must 'detach ourselves from the senses', and that a bodiless being may have doubts. If one holds that the person is the *human being* it is unclear that there will be any room for Descartes' doubt about the material world.

3. Knowledge and action: For Descartes 'to know reality is to have a correct picture within of outer reality'. One might instead take as one's paradigm of someone who knows something someone who acts with confidence.

4. An 'absolute conception': it will be objected that unless we think of knowledge as being something that underlies confident action we will be committed to the conclusion that the individual's picture of the world is inevitably coloured by her own reactions to it. The Cartesian picture of the self as a being that is radically distinct from the bodily being may have its deepest roots here: in an image of real knowledge as involving a pure mirroring of a situation. But perhaps we can resist that image.

1
Descartes: The Self and the World

1. Dualism and materialism

The French philosopher René Descartes (1596–1650) has had a profound and lasting impact on philosophical views of the self and its knowledge of the world. The ideas that are responsible for that impact can be found in the short, and highly readable, book *Meditations on the First Philosophy*.

Descartes' view of what a person is might be summarized in this way. A live human being is composed of two parts: a material body and a non-material mind. It is the latter – the mind, or, as we might say, the soul – that is the real person. For it is here that mental states occur; and it is these states – rather than the physical states of my body – that are fundamental to my life as a person. During my present life the mind 'inhabits' the body, in the sense that it is closely causally linked with this particular body. But there is no difficulty in the idea that I – that is, my mind – should continue to exist in a completely non-bodily form after the destruction of my body.

Something like this view has always had, and continues to have, a strong hold on the thinking of a great many people. But, while the view was not invented by Descartes, it is his presentation and defence of it that has had the most powerful impact on subsequent philosophical discussions of this issue. Within twentieth-century western philosophy that impact has been largely negative, in the sense that contemporary views of what a person is have developed as a reaction to Descartes. While the reaction has taken a variety of forms, English-speaking philosophy of the last fifty years or so has been dominated by one form or another of 'materialism': the view, roughly, that the only things that exist are material substances of the kind spoken of in the

1

physical sciences. Talk of non-material minds or souls is a myth. There is no more to a person than his or her body.

That very general 'materialist' idea can be developed in different ways. On the one hand, we have views that insist that anger, for example, is not, as the dualist suggests, some inner state of a non-material mind that *lies behind* the overt behaviour in which the anger finds expression; the anger simply *is* the overt, bodily behaviour. On the other hand, we have views according to which mental states are, in fact, *physical states of the brain*. That is not to deny that people have minds. It is simply to argue that the mind is a particular physical organ of the body. Variants of this view have such a powerful grip on much contemporary thought that the terms 'mind' and 'brain' are often used interchangeably. Some readers may have to remind themselves, particularly when we are considering Descartes' view, that it is only according to one – though currently dominant – philosophical view that the terms 'mind' and 'brain' refer to the same thing.

2. The distinctness of the human soul from the body

These more recent developments will be considered in later chapters. Our concern in this chapter is with Descartes and his *Meditations*. In the 'Dedication' of that work Descartes says that he has two principal aims. The first is to demonstrate 'the distinctness of the human soul from the body', and the second to demonstrate that 'God may be more easily and certainly known than the things of the world' (Descartes, 1641, p. 66). Now in Descartes' thought these tasks are connected in a surprising fashion. We might summarize the position in this way:

> I am something quite distinct from any material being. I lie outside the world of material things: the world of tables, trees, mountains and so on. And my beliefs about that world are based on data that, as I suppose, I receive from it by way of my senses. Thus, I do not have direct contact with that world. It is, then, only through a demonstration of the existence of a truthful and benevolent God that I can have any grounds for believing that there *is* a material world at all, or that that world is at all as I normally take it to be.

It will be worth exploring in some detail the reasoning that lies behind this view.

The 'First Meditation' opens with the following observation:

> Several years have now elapsed since I first became aware that I had accepted, even from my youth, many false opinions for true, and

that consequently what I afterwards based on such principles was highly doubtful; and from that time I was convinced of the necessity of undertaking once in my life to rid myself of all the opinions I had adopted, and of commencing anew the work of building from the foundation, if I desired to establish a firm and abiding superstructure in the sciences. (Descartes, 1641, p. 79)

Descartes decided, then, that he must doubt everything that it is possible for him to doubt. If anything is left, that will form a secure foundation on which basis he can begin to reconstruct a system of knowledge.

Which of Descartes' beliefs are open to possible doubt? He suggests first that all of those beliefs that he has, up till now, accepted as most certain have been dependent in some way on the senses. He notes too that his senses have sometimes deceived him. But that, he suggests, does not cast doubt on many of his former beliefs; for only a madman would conclude from the fact that his senses have sometimes deceived him that it is possible that his senses have deceived him about *everything*.

Descartes notes next that he has often dreamed that he was dressed and sitting by the fire, as he now is, when in fact he was lying undressed in bed. On reflection, it seems clear to him that 'there exist no certain marks by which the state of waking can ever be distinguished from sleep' (Descartes, 1641, p. 81). Does not the possibility that he might now be asleep and dreaming show that there is room for doubt about the great majority of his familiar beliefs? Well, it will, Descartes argues, leave a fair amount standing. Even if he is now dreaming that he is dressed and sitting by the fire it must still be the case that he has *in reality* had experience of things of the kind about which he is dreaming. Further, whether he is awake or asleep he can still be quite certain that, for example, two and three make five, and a square has four sides.

Some might wonder whether Descartes' confidence is not misplaced here. But this is of no great importance, for Descartes does not let matters rest there. He suggests that the most effective way to call into question all of those beliefs about which there is the smallest room for doubt will be to imagine that there is a malignant demon of unlimited powers who does all that he can to deceive him. It is in this spirit that he writes:

I will suppose that the sky, the air, the earth, colours, figures, sounds, and all external things, are nothing better than the illusions of dreams, by means of which this being has laid snares for my credulity; I will consider myself as without hands, eyes, flesh, blood, or any of the senses, and as falsely believing that I am possessed of these. (Descartes, 1641, p. 84)

Descartes is not here claiming to believe that there *is* such a malignant demon, and that he himself does not have hands, eyes, and so on. His point is simply that, as things now stand with him, he cannot prove that there *isn't*. And so long as he cannot prove this, he has to admit that it is possible that he is wrong in almost everything that he has, up till now, believed.

Some modern readers may find that this talk of 'malignant demons' creates an obstacle to their entering completely into the spirit of Descartes' thinking. Contemporary versions of his reasoning speak instead of the possibility that I am a brain in a vat: a brain that is being fed wholly false information about the world by a mad scientist. While this supposition will not take us quite to where Descartes would like us to go, little harm will be done if, at this point, you feel more at home with 'mad scientists' than with 'evil demons'.

Descartes believes that with the hypothesis of the malignant demon he has made out the best possible case for doubt. If he cannot prove that he is not in the hands of such a demon then he can have no confidence in almost any of his former beliefs. If, however, he can find just one thing about which there is no possible room for doubt he will, perhaps, be able to take this as a firm foundation on which to build:

> Archimedes, that he might transport the entire globe from the place it occupied to another, demanded only a point that was firm and immovable; so also, I shall be entitled to entertain the highest expectations, if I am fortunate enough to discover only one thing that is certain and indubitable. (Descartes, 1641, p. 85)

Descartes finds what he needs in his experience of himself:

> Doubtless, then, I exist, since I am deceived; and, let him deceive me as he may, he can never bring it about that I am nothing, so long as I shall be conscious that I am something. (Descartes, 1641, p. 86)

This, then, is Descartes' secure foundation: his conviction that he himself exists could not possibly be mistaken.

How can he build on this foundation? Descartes argues that on the basis of what he has so far established he can prove that 'I am entirely and truly distinct from my body, and may exist without it' (Descartes, 1641, pp. 132–3), and that there is a powerful and benevolent God.

While it is the second of these conclusions that is most important to his project of finding a secure foundation for knowledge, it is the first that is crucial to our concerns in this book. Of a number of arguments Descartes presents for this claim about what he is, perhaps the most important is this:

> ...because, on the one hand, I have a clear and distinct idea of myself, in as far as I am only a thinking and unextended thing, and as, on the other hand, I possess a distinct idea of body, in as far as it is only an extended and unthinking thing, it is certain that I (that is, my mind, by which I am when I am) am entirely and truly distinct from my body, and may exist without it. (Descartes, 1641, pp. 132–3)

The passage calls for a comment on Descartes' terminology. When Descartes speaks of himself as a 'thinking thing' he is using the term 'thinking' in an unusually broad way. In another work he explains that by 'thinking' he means 'all that which so takes place in us that we of ourselves are immediately conscious of it' (Descartes, 1644, p. 167). He adds that he includes under the heading 'thinking': understanding, willing, imagining and perceiving. We might say that by the phrase 'a thinking thing' he means 'a being that has mental states'. Now Descartes takes it to be clear that this – that he has mental states – is what is fundamental to his nature. If I suffered an irreversible loss of consciousness – an irreversible loss of all mental states – there would, it might be said, be little sense in which I would continue to exist at all.

Descartes' argument for the conclusion that he – that is, his mind – is entirely and truly distinct from his body is, then, this. I can form a conception of myself – conjure up a picture of myself – as a being that doubts, imagines, desires and so on without including anything bodily in that picture. For example, I can imagine what it would be like to find myself having experiences just as if I was seeing this desk and computer screen, thinking about this philosophical problem, feeling emotions of anger, fear or joy, and yet not having a body. We can conclude, Descartes suggests, that the relation between him – that is, his mind – and his body is not like that between, for example, a smile and the face that the smile is on. The smile is not 'entirely and truly distinct' from the face; as we see when we recognize that we cannot form a clear and distinct idea of a smile quite independently of any idea of a face with a smile on it. In that sense, we do not know what it would be for there to be a smile without a face. By contrast, Descartes insists, he is quite clear what it would be for him to exist without a body. In that sense the real person is quite distinct from his or her body.

In Descartes' support, we might note that significant numbers of people claim to have undergone experiences in which they have 'come apart from their body' in just the kind of way Descartes imagines. They claim, and clearly believe, that, for a period, they left their body and observed it, and other material things, from some other point in space. Now in one sense, it does not, for the purposes of Descartes' argument, matter too much whether one actually believes that such things have happened. What is important is simply that we understand such stories: they are not self-contradictory or unintelligible in the way in which stories about 'five-sided triangles' or 'a smile without a face' would be.

It might be objected that it does not follow from the fact that we can *imagine* something – that, for example, I can imagine existing apart from my body – that it is possible in reality; and surely *that* is the crucial thing. I can imagine – conjure up a picture of myself – existing without a heart; it does not follow from that that it is in practice possible for a human being to exist without a heart.

To respond to this protest we need to distinguish between different kinds of 'impossibility'. Compare the 'impossibility' of there being a smile without a face, or a five-sided triangle, with the 'impossibility' of a human being levitating or existing without a heart. The contrast between these cases is sometimes expressed by saying that the first two are 'logically impossible' while the second two are only 'physically impossible'. It is part of what we mean by a 'smile' that it is something that appears on a face; and part of what we mean by a 'triangle' that it has three, and so not five, sides. Something that did not appear on a face, or that did not have just three sides, would not count as a 'smile' or a 'triangle'. It is sometimes said that even God could not bring about what is logically impossible; though it might be better to say that while God can do anything, whatever he did it would not constitute, for example, 'producing a five-sided triangle'. By contrast, while a human life is, of course, crucially causally dependent on a functioning heart, there is, it seems, no *incoherence* in the idea that a living human being might lack a heart: if God is not constrained by the laws of physics he might produce something that was correctly described in that way. Now what Descartes hopes to have proved is that the connection between the mind and body is merely causal; there is no *incoherence* in the idea of the one continuing to exist after the destruction of the other. In that sense they are distinct entities: as the arms and the legs of a man are distinct entities, while the smile and the face, or the vase and its shape, are not.

Descartes' conclusion, then, is this: I am a non-material mind or soul, which thinks, feels, wills and so on, and which – while closely causally linked with a particular material body during this life – is a quite distinct entity and so could, in principle, survive the destruction of that body.

3. Descartes' dualism and our normal thought

In support of this understanding of what a person is we might appeal to a variety of other factors. We might, for example, consider the kind of knowledge that I have of, on the one hand, my own mental states and, on the other, the mental states of others. Descartes notes that, while in the depths of his doubt, he can be quite certain that he 'thinks' – that is to say, doubts, imagines, desire and so on – even though he knows nothing of his body, including whether he even has one. This feature of Descartes' argument is reflected in the familiar fact that my knowledge of my own mental states is, apparently, quite independent of any knowledge that I have about the state or activities of my body. For example, my knowledge that I am in acute pain is not dependent on any observation of my contorted face or anguished cries. Of my own sensations I have, it seems, an infallible knowledge that is not mediated by any knowledge of the material world. Conversely, I do, it seems, never have direct access to the mental states of others. While I can, perhaps, form reasonable conjectures about what you are feeling on the basis of your behaviour, I never actually observe your anger or pain itself. Anger and pain are, as we put it, 'inner states'. They are 'inner' not simply in the sense of being physically below the surface of your skin: the brain surgeon no more directly observes another's pain or anger than the rest of us do. They are 'inner' in the more radical sense that they are states of a kind that cannot be seen or touched; they are, in short, 'inner' in the sense of being non-material states.

Consider too the knowledge that I have of *who* I am. Confronted with a certain car I tell which car it is – that it is the car that I have owned for the last eight years – by noticing its physical features: a battered Mercedes of that quite distinctive, and absurd, shade of blue, and so on. By contrast, when I wake in the morning I know who I am without first taking a glance at my body: 'noticing the physical features of this body' is quite irrelevant to my ability to say that it is me – David

Cockburn – who has just woken up and is thinking about the day ahead. 'Knowing who I am' is something quite distinct from 'knowing which human body this is'; and so the real me – that which the word 'I' refers to – must be something quite distinct from this human body.

Reflection on the experience that I have of my own mental states and that which I have of the mental states of others seems, then, to support the radical contrast Descartes draws between the *mental* and the *physical*. While the mind is, no doubt, closely causally linked with the body, it must be acknowledged to be a distinct, non-material, realm.

Considerations of a rather different kind might be found by reflecting on the *importance* that we take people to have. We have towards human beings a whole range of attitudes and responses of kinds that we do not have towards inanimate objects. In particular circumstances we feel towards another pity, resentment, fear, admiration and so on; and most of us assume that such responses are sometimes in place. Is it not clear, however, that such responses can only be in place if the being to which we are responding is not simply material in nature? It is true, of course, that the feelings that are in place when confronted with a material object may depend on its particular structure. For example, some material objects – say, a rumbling volcano – are appropriate objects of fear. But what makes it that is simply the fact that, because of its physical structure, it is likely to bring about certain effects that are dangerous to human beings. Now the quite special range of attitudes that we take to be in place towards other people cannot be made intelligible in comparable terms. One cannot, for example, show why pity is an appropriate response to someone writhing on the ground – as we say, in obvious pain – by pointing to likely physical consequences of what is now happening. Our idea that responses in this range are appropriate seems to be dependent on an assumption of a different kind: an assumption that there is something going on here that is radically different from any of the physical changes that are taking place inside the person's body.

Perhaps this kind of point has clearest application in cases in the following area. We praise and blame people, we feel gratitude and resentment towards people, on account of things that they have done. These practices involve the idea that people are in some sense *responsible* for what they do. That is to say, presumably, they involve the idea that what a person does is not the product of a mechanical sequence of causes and effects – as the eruption of the volcano is. No doubt the movement of the person's arm was caused by the contraction of his muscles, and this in turn was caused by certain impulses in the nerves. But if this physical chain of causes and effects stretched back indefinitely we would seem to lose all sense of the idea that the *person* was responsible for what happened. Apart from anything else, if there was not a clear sense in which he could have acted other than he did (as the volcano could not, I take it, have 'acted other than it did') then praise and blame would, surely, be quite inappropriate responses to him. Our normal responses to human actions are, then, only in place if somewhere along this chain we come to something that is not simply another physical change with physical causes: if, that is, the sequence was initiated by a change in some entity – a mind – that lies outside the material realm of mechanical causes and effects.

In contrast with some of the earlier considerations, no argument of this form could show that pain, anger and so on are non-material states of a non-material mind. The point raised in the last paragraph would, if sound, only show that this is an assumption on which our normal relations with each other crucially depend. Still, one might hope that the truth about what we are will turn out to be reasonably consistent with what is most important in our normal thought about each other.

4. Knowledge of 'the things of the world'

Let us return to Descartes. We need not pursue his proofs of the existence of God, except to note that these are dependent only on what Descartes knows about his own mind. (Readers who wish to do so can find these in *Meditations* III and V.) What is of importance to us is the question of what leads Descartes to say that 'God may be more easily and certainly known than the things of the world' – for the answer to this question is closely linked with his understanding of what he is. Descartes has concluded that he is 'precisely speaking, only a thinking thing, that is, a mind'. He has argued that this means that he is quite distinct from his body; where this means that there is no difficulty in the idea that he could have existed even though he had no body. That is not to deny that he – that is, his mind – is *causally connected* with his body. Activities in my mind cause parts of my body to move: as when I raise my arm. And the mind receives impressions from the various different parts of the body: the eyes, the ears, the hands and so on. Now it is on the basis of these 'impressions', or 'ideas', that I construct my picture of the material world.

It is important to note, as Descartes himself does, that in thinking of himself in this way he has moved away from a picture of himself that he had before he embarked on his meditations. He used to think, he tells us, that his body was a part, or perhaps even the whole, of himself (Descartes, 1641, p. 129). With that, he used to think that this being which he himself was, 'was placed among many others'. That is to say, he took himself to be a being that was in the same world as, and in constant interaction with, material objects such as tables and chairs and trees. As the result of his meditations, however, he has come to think of himself, and so his position in the world, very differently. This change is reflected in the way in which he speaks, in a passage quoted above, of all material things as '*external* things'. He has, no doubt, always thought of tables, trees and so on as things of a quite different kind from himself. To that thought, however, he has now added the thought that, in an important sense, he and they exist in different worlds. While causally connected with it, he himself is not a *part* of the world of extended, tangible beings. Thus, he is dependent for his knowledge of that world on messages – what he calls 'ideas' – that he receives from it.

It is now not difficult to see why Descartes holds that 'God may be more easily and certainly known than the things of the world'. If my beliefs about tables, trees and so on are all based on certain states of my mind – that is, on ideas that I assume to be *effects* of those things – there is room for the question: with what justification do I assume that these ideas *are* caused by material things that resemble them? Descartes, having proved to his satisfaction that there is a powerful and benevolent God, has a ready answer to this question. Since I have:

> a very strong inclination to believe that those ideas arise from corporeal objects, I do not see how he [God] could be vindicated from the charge of deceit, if in truth they proceeded from any other source, or were produced by other causes than corporeal things: and accordingly it must be concluded, that corporeal objects exist. (Descartes, 1641, p. 134)

Of course, we will only agree that 'God may be more easily and certainly known than the things of the world' if we accept that Descartes has established the existence of God, and that there is no other possible justification for thinking that our ideas are caused by corporeal things. However, my aim here is not to defend these steps in Descartes' argument but simply to attain a clear view of the structure of his thought. God serves to bridge the gap between my knowledge of myself and my beliefs about the world: the gap that opened up when he reached the conclusion that 'I am entirely and truly distinct from my body'.

5. Myself and others

We have been considering Descartes' conception of himself and his relation to the world of material things. We must consider also the implications of his account for our understanding of the individual's relation to other people. We catch a glimpse of Descartes' understanding of the social dimension of human life in the way in which his philosophical project is presented to us. Where other philosophers have offered us dialogues he offers us 'meditations'. And it should be sufficiently clear from what I have said why, in Descartes' view, the argument he presents is one that each of us must go through for herself. In doubting the existence of the world of tables and trees Descartes is, while he does not state this explicitly, almost inevitably doubting the existence of other people; for his beliefs about them are, we might suppose, dependent on his beliefs about their 'bodies'. There would, then, be something distinctly odd in the idea that Descartes and a colleague might work through the early stages of Descartes' argument *together.*

That point is closely linked with the fact that it is clear that Descartes will not, at this stage of his argument, regard the fact that a 'trustworthy person' told him something as adequate grounds for accepting what he was told. It is connected too with the understanding of what he himself is that emerges in later Meditations. Just as I am not, on this understanding, part of the same world as that of tables and trees so I am not part of the same world as that of other people. Indeed, there is a clear sense in which, on this picture, I am one step further removed from other people than I am from material things. For just as my knowledge of the material world is mediated by my knowledge of myself, so my knowledge of another is mediated by my knowledge of the material world. Just as I know about the tree only through the 'ideas' it causes in my mind, so I know about your mind only through the effects it has on the material world: most immediately, through the behavioural effects it has on your body. The way in which Descartes' image of 'the self' makes my knowledge of the material world problematic is, then, reflected, in a more extreme form, in a way in which it makes my knowledge of other people problematic. Descartes, as we have seen, overcomes the first problem by an appeal to the idea of a powerful and benevolent God; and, while he does not discuss the matter, he could, presumably, introduce God in exactly the same way in relation to the second problem. But is there any way in which we might respond to the second problem without such an appeal to God?

We will take up that question in Chapter 3. Before coming to that, however, we must consider a way in which certain forms of experience that some claim to have had might be thought to provide support for the view of the self that Descartes defends.

Further reading

Descartes' view is presented in its clearest form in his *Meditations on the First Philosophy*. For a brief introduction to Descartes, which focuses on his account of what he is, see John Cottingham, *Descartes*. A more detailed, and very accessible, survey and discussion of Descartes' philosophy as a whole, with particular reference to his views on mind and body, is Anthony Kenny, *Descartes: a Study of his Philosophy*. A more advanced, and very stimulating, discussion is Bernard Williams, *Descartes: the Project of Pure Enquiry*. A useful, detailed discussion of dualism can be found in Part I of Peter Smith and O.R. Jones, *The Philosophy of Mind*. Gilbert Ryle's *The Concept of Mind* is an enormously influential onslaught on what he calls 'Descartes' myth'; chapter 1 presents a clear picture of the kind of confusion that Ryle suggests is involved in Descartes' account. While dualism of the kind Descartes defends is not at all fashionable in the philosophical world today it does have a few defenders. A notable example is Richard Swinburne; see, for example, his *The Evolution of the Soul*.

2
The Cartesian Soul and the Paranormal

1. Imagination and the self

In Chapter 1 I presented Descartes' argument for the conclusion that he – that is, his mind – is entirely and truly distinct from his body in this way:

> I can form a conception of myself – conjure up a picture of myself – as a being that doubts, imagines, desires and so on without including anything bodily in that picture. For example, I can imagine what it would be like to find myself having experiences just as if I was seeing this desk and computer screen, thinking about this philosophical problem, feeling emotions of anger, fear or joy, and yet not having a body. We can conclude, Descartes suggests, that the relation between him – that is, his mind – and his body is not like that between, for example, a smile and the face that the smile is on. The smile is not 'entirely and truly distinct' from the face; as we see when we recognize that we cannot form a clear and distinct idea of a smile quite independently of any idea of a face with a smile on it. In that sense, we do not know what it would be for there to be a smile without a face. By contrast, Descartes insists, he is quite clear what it would be for him to exist without a body. In that sense the real person is quite distinct from his or her body.

I considered the natural objection that one cannot move from claims about what we can imagine to conclusions about what is possible in reality. I responded by drawing a distinction between what is merely 'physically' impossible and what is 'logically' impossible: suggesting that it is the latter notion that is important for Descartes' conclusion, and that the fact that we can imagine something *does* establish that it is logically possible. But those remarks may have been too quick.

Consider the question: does it follow from the fact that you can draw something that what you have drawn is possible in reality? One might reply that while in one sense of 'possible' it does not follow, in another sense of 'possible' it does. But now consider the picture on the Front cover of this book. Are we to say that the difficulty in the idea of a closed, continuously falling stream of water is 'merely physical'? That, clearly, does not do justice to the matter. The idea of such a stream is incoherent, in something like the sense in which the idea of a four-sided triangle is incoherent. Yet we have a picture of it! (If you are inclined to say that the difficulty is simply that water can't flow uphill think, and look, again.)

We might conclude: it does not follow from the fact that something can be drawn that it is, in any sense, possible in reality. Or we might express the point by saying that this is not really a picture of a closed, continuously falling stream of water; it is simply a picture that one might be tempted to describe in that way if one didn't think too hard about it. It does not much matter in which of these ways one expresses the point. Either way, it must be conceded that no sure guide to what is possible – even to what is logically possible – is to be found in what can be depicted on paper.

An exactly analogous point applies to the imagination. It does not follow from the fact that I can conjure up images that I am inclined to describe as 'me coming apart from my body' that those words are a coherent description of some possibility. The imagination provides no such short cut to substantial philosophical conclusions about what a person is. There is no escaping the hard work that some philosophers put us through here: the hard work, for example, that will be the substance of this book.

None of that is to say that Descartes' view of the person is *wrong*. It is to say, at most, that one of his arguments for that view is not valid. But the pull of Descartes' thinking is powerful. We can, I think, see its power in the attraction of certain forms of argument that are closely akin to Descartes': arguments that appeal, not to the possibility of *imagining* coming apart from my body, but to the experience some claim to have had of actually *having done so*. We must now turn to such arguments.

2. Dualism, science and out-of-body experiences

It is now widely assumed that the most crucial questions about what a person is are questions which are to be answered by appeal to empirical evidence. Descartes, it is suggested, went wrong in supposing that he could establish what he was simply by a process of philosophical reflection. It is hard scientific data, not a priori theorizing, that is needed if we are to discover what we are. It is, further, widely assumed, at least within certain quarters, that the empirical evidence points fairly unambiguously towards a 'materialist' account of the person. Scientific discoveries, it is said, now strongly suggest that all the phenomena of human life can be explained entirely in the terms employed by the physical sciences: that is to say, without postulating any non-material 'mind' or 'soul' of the kind that is central to Cartesianism. We should, then, conclude that a person simply *is* a complex physical organism.

We will be considering those arguments in later chapters. In this chapter I want to consider what we might call 'the other side' of the contemporary debate. It is suggested by some that proper attention to all the available data will not push us unambiguously towards the materialist camp. For, it is argued, there are well-established phenomena that *cannot* be explained in 'physical' terms. The relevant phenomena may be slightly elusive; and they are of a kind to which the current scientific temperament tends to be blind. But if we pay proper attention to them we may find ourselves forced to conclude that there is more to be said for the Cartesian picture than is generally acknowledged by the established scientific community. I want to consider these claims by focusing on one kind of phenomenon that is sometimes appealed to here: that of 'out-of-body experiences' (OBEs).

A considerable number of people have had experiences in which it has seemed to them that, for a period, they left their body. There are a variety of circumstances in which people report having had such experiences. One of the most striking, and most closely investigated, are those in which a person has been 'close to death'. An individual who, for a period, showed (more or less) no behavioural or physiological signs of life, on being resuscitated reports having left her body while 'unconscious'. She insists that she observed the room, or indeed some other place, from a position external to her body. Furthermore, people who have had this experience are, it is claimed, sometimes able to give accurate reports of events that were taking place while they were apparently unconscious and that could not have been observed from the point where their body was at the time. This, it is suggested, provides corroboration of their reports. It is not simply that it *seemed* to her as if she left her body: as it might seem to someone in a dream. We have real independent evidence that the person did leave her body and observe the world from a point external to it. And that is to say, we have real empirical evidence that, as Descartes maintained, a person is something distinct from his or her body.

I want to suggest that, at the very least, a considerable amount of work needs to be done at a number of points if it is to be shown that phenomena of this kind bear on our picture of ourselves in anything like the ways suggested. I should stress that I will not be calling into question any of the empirical data appealed to. My suggestion will, rather, be that enormous care is needed in taking even a first step beyond that data. Our thinking here is, I will suggest, coloured by a certain imagery of which we need to be suspicious.

A feature of the phenomenon that impresses some commentators is the fact that these people report having had thoughts, feelings, visual sensations, and so on while in a state in which they showed no physiological signs of life. I will set to one side here any worries that we might have about whether they could, in offering these reports, be suffering from some delusion of memory. I will assume, that is, that the person did have some form of experience while, for example, her brain scan was flat. What bearing would this surprising fact have on our understanding of what we are? One thing it might show is that what we experience at a particular time is not totally dependent on the state of our brain at that time. While that will, no doubt, come as a surprise to many, we need to draw a sharp distinction between *this* question – the question of what my consciousness is *dependent on* – and the question of what I am: the question, that is, of what it *is* that is conscious. Consider an analogy. We normally assume that how well a car goes is crucially dependent on the state of the engine. Suppose, however, that we were presented with startling evidence strongly suggesting that the performance of a car could be affected by influences of a kind that are totally alien to contemporary science. Would such a discovery do anything at all to suggest that my car is not that familiar thing with four wheels, a roof, and so on? Would it support the idea that it is possible for my car to live on after the disintegration of the extended, tangible thing parked outside? This, I take it, is obvious nonsense.

Now on the face of it, it is the same with people. It is one thing to ask what a person's states are *dependent on*. That is a question for science. It is quite another to ask what those states are states *of*; to ask, that is, what it is that thinks, sees, is happy or sad and so on. Whether the answer to the first question is 'the brain' or something quite different is totally irrelevant to the second question. Neither way will it affect the suggestion that it is the human being that thinks, sees and so on. OBEs cannot in this way give any support to the idea that the person – the 'real me' – is something distinct from this extended, tangible being.

But what of the accurate reports, which it is claimed some are able to offer, of what was happening at the time in places not observable from the bed where the human being was lying? Do these not demonstrate that the individual 'left her body' for a period; and so that the 'real person' is something quite distinct from this bodily being?

This would be moving a bit too rapidly. The facts so far described are quite consistent with the suggestion that the patient was able to give these reports as a result of signals picked up while she was located where she appeared to be: namely, in bed. Now it might be objected that this talk of 'signals' does not really do justice to the way in which the individual's *perspective on the world* was for a period from a point external to her body. It is not merely that she knows what was happening, say, next door. For a period she *saw* things from a point in the next-door room; or, at least, it now seems to her that she did. Does not this strongly suggest that part of the patient was 'outside her body' for that period?

Well, even if we agree that it does suggest this the argument would still require a further step in order to get us to the conclusion that what left the body was the 'real person'. If my eyes were on the ends of long stalks I could observe what was going on next door. I would, no doubt, when particularly absorbed in what I was seeing, half think of myself as being in that room; or perhaps even, momentarily, come to believe that that was where I was. None of this would put any pressure on us to say that I really was next door: it was one small part of me, not *me*, that was next door.

I should stress that I am not, with this talk of 'eyes on stalks', offering an alternative explanation of 'out-of-body experiences': I am not suggesting that some form of immaterial eyes are going out on immaterial stalks. I am simply pointing out that we cannot just take it for granted – as the dualist appeal to OBEs appears to – that a person is situated at the point from which he or she sees the world.

Nevertheless, it might be said, a dualist view of persons *can* provide an explanation of the observed phenomena in a way in which no (remotely plausible) alternative view can. Thus, at least until we have an adequate explanation consistent with the view that the bodily being is the real person, these phenomena should be regarded as grounds for accepting the dualist view.

In responding to this argument I should concede first that I have no idea whatsoever how these phenomena might be explained. I spoke of 'signals' that the patient, in her bed, might be picking up. Let us suppose, however, that we have good reason for ruling out any such explanation; *nothing*, at least of the kind now recognized by physics, is passing from the relevant point in space to the patient in bed. We are left thinking either in terms of the transmission of something *not* recognized by physics, or in terms of action at a distance: what happens at one place (the event on which she is able to report) is affecting the patient even though there is *no mechanism whatsoever* that connects the events with the patient.

Let us now compare the paucity of my 'explanation' with how the dualist theory would explain such veridical OBE reports. We are perhaps inclined to see it like this: 'On the dualist theory I am something quite distinct from this body. This opens the possibility of explaining veridical OBE reports in terms of the fact that the individual left her body and observed the world from a position external to it.' Traditional philosophical dualism, of the kind associated with Descartes, does not, I think, leave room for such an explanation since it does not leave room for the idea that the 'real me' has any spatial location. Thus, Descartes writes: 'I thence concluded that I was a substance whose whole essence or nature consists only in thinking, and which, that it may exist, has need of no place...' (Descartes, 1637, p. 27). On *this* view, then, I cannot leave my body since I was never in it! I will not pursue the question of whether some other form of dualism could leave room for the idea that the 'real me' has spatial location, since I believe there are further problems.

Perhaps the most notorious objection to dualism concerns the question of the interaction between mind and body. To the extent that one holds that the 'real me' is something quite different in kind from this extended, solid entity, one appears to rule out the possibility of there being any intelligible mechanism that links what happens in the one substance with what happens in the other. Descartes, in my view rightly, was apparently quite unimpressed by this supposed objection to dualism. My point at the moment, however, is simply this. My 'explanation' of what is going on in OBEs spoke lamely of 'signals' or of 'action at a distance'. Now that *is* pretty lame; indeed, it might be said that it is hardly an explanation at all. But the dualist's 'explanation' of veridical OBE reports is going to contain a gap of exactly the same kind; for the dualist's 'explanation' of *everything* that people do and experience is going to contain a gap of this kind. Thus, in the explanation of *any* visual experience the dualist can only speak, equally lamely, of an event in the non-material mind somehow being brought about by a material object. We cannot, then, argue that the OBE phenomenon gives us reason to move towards a two-component picture of persons on *these* grounds: on grounds of explanatory adequacy.

One further point can be made here. The suggestion is that veridical OBE reports support some kind of dualism because dualism would allow us to explain the reports in terms of the fact that the individual was for a period located at the relevant place. Now, in normal circumstances we do, of course, take the fact that I was at a certain place at a certain time as explaining the knowledge that I have of what happened there. In a particular case, however, this would be no explanation at all if it were discovered that I had lost my eyes, ears and so on before going there. Would it, then, be an explanation if I had, temporarily, 'lost my body'?

3. A tension in our thought

In the previous section I threw every argument I could think of at the suggestion that 'out-of-body experiences' might provide some support for a dualist view of people. It is, I think, relatively easy to see how these arguments might be adapted to respond to analogous appeals to certain other paranormal phenomena. Now I should stress that my aim here is not to deny that there are paranormal phenomena; nor that they might show us some pretty interesting things. My interest is simply in what seem to me to be serious misunderstandings about *what* they might show us about what we are.

I have found that those who appeal to paranormal phenomena in the way that I have been criticizing are generally little impressed by the criticisms. This is, I think, in part a reflection of the huge prestige of science within our culture. It is taken to be obvious that the really important questions about what we are are to be settled by appeal to 'scientific' evidence; and so it is difficult to get a serious hearing for any attempt to suggest that the evidence may not be relevant in quite the ways assumed.

But I want briefly to draw attention to another factor that may be at work here. We are *all*, I think, tempted to interpret the reported phenomena in terms of the individual 'leaving her body'. Many will no doubt feel that it *must* be quite easy to meet the points I have made since, it will be said, this interpretation of the phenomena is so obviously the most natural one. Now I suspect that this feeling reflects, in part, a curious ease with which we slide between two quite different pictures of what a person is. We can see this by focusing on one of the objections that I raised in the previous section.

Assume that we have strong evidence for the claim that for a period the individual's visual perspective on the world was from a point outside the physical body. My question is: should this lead us to say that for that period the person was (or it is likely that she was) situated at a point outside her body? To draw this conclusion we would need to have independent grounds for the following claim: people are (generally) situated at that point from which their visual perspective on the world is. Without this claim, the inference is quite unjustified. Do we have any grounds for it?

On the face of it we do. We might say that we have overwhelming grounds for the claim that – with the exception of cases involving mirrors, television and the like (which we will assume can be dealt with somehow) – people are always situated at that point from which their visual perspective on the world is. Now I think that is right. Leaving aside for the moment the phenomena we are dealing with – namely OBEs – this seems to be a very well-supported universal truth. But it is only a well-supported truth in so far as it is assumed that people are *human beings*. For what we seem to have strong evidence for is the claim that: human beings – these visible, tangible entities with arms and legs and heads – are always situated at that point from which their visual perspective on the world is. Now this is no use at all for the person who wants to use OBEs to establish some form of dualism. For the whole point of his argument is to challenge the claim that people are human beings: his conclusion is that the real person is something distinct from the bodily human being. That is: his conclusion is inconsistent with an assumption that he needs to make in order to reach it! Something has gone badly wrong.

So the question is now: if one thinks that the person is something distinct from the human being – as one must if one is going to claim that in these cases 'people do leave their bodies' – what grounds can one have for the claim that people are (generally) situated at that point from which their visual perspective on the world is? What one needs is the following: people are generally situated inside human beings. Assuming that we are dealing with a form of dualism within which this *makes sense*, it is not at all clear what could count as evidence for it. At any rate, until we are shown how this claim might be supported we appear to have no grounds at all for moving from the suggestion that 'the individual's perspective on the world was, for a period, from a point of view external to this body' to the idea that 'the individual was, for that period, situated at that point'. The idea that the 'real person' is the crying, talking, sleeping, walking human being is quite untouched by these phenomena.

As I said, I think that we fail to see this because we slide between two quite different pictures of what a person is. We can only think that we have grounds for a claim that our argument needs – the claim that people are generally situated at that point from which their visual perspective on the world is – in so far as we picture the person as being the human being. But someone whose aim is to prove that the real person is something distinct from the visible, tangible human being can hardly use an argument that is only valid on the assumption that people are human beings. I say 'can hardly'. My suspicion is that this is precisely what most of us are inclined to do.

4. Value, science and the immaterial

My claim has not been that we do not *have* to draw from the reported phenomena the conclusions that commonly are drawn. It is, rather, that further work needs to be done at a number of points if it is to be shown that the phenomena give us *any reason at all* to draw these conclusions. The idea that they give us such a reason is, I have suggested, dependent on an illusion that I have tried to expose. Unfortunately, following an argument in which one can find no flaw (as I, no doubt optimistically, count on you finding no flaw in mine!) is, by itself, seldom sufficient to dispel an illusion: any more than measuring the lines in the Muller–Lyer illusion is, by itself, sufficient to destroy the illusion that one is longer than the other (see Figure 2.1). But perhaps the hold of the inferences which I am criticizing can be weakened by further reflection on the kind of *importance* that it might be supposed attaches to the debate about the Cartesian view of the self.

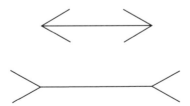

Figure 2.1   The Muller–Lyer illusion

Much of the interest in parapsychological phenomena is, I think, motivated by something like the following thought:

> As soon as one grants that a person is an extended, tangible, observable being – a being that exists in the world of stones, trees and mountains – one is committing oneself to the view that the world as described by modern physics is *the* world. This has dramatic implications for our conception of ourselves. For example, it rules out the possibility of our thinking of ourselves as in any way responsible for what we do; what we do must be accepted as being the product of the impersonal mechanisms described by the physicist. More generally, the idea that we are fundamentally 'spiritual' beings – beings that have the kind of value traditionally associated with talk of 'the soul' – must be abandoned.

This kind of argument will be of considerable importance in later chapters. But it is worth saying a little about it now.

The idea that value can seep into the world through the cracks in physics has a long history. A question that can and needs to be asked, quite independently of any investigation into whether there are such cracks, is this: why should it be thought that whatever seeps in through such cracks is of any value? Consider the question of responsibility. Suppose that we could accept that a person is essentially an 'immaterial' being. How would this help the idea that we are in some sense responsible for what we do? If the claim that something is 'immaterial' simply means that you cannot see it, touch it, weigh it, and so on, then it needs to be shown why an immaterial being should not be every bit as determined by 'impersonal mechanisms' as a material being can be. The rigid laws to which it is subject won't, perhaps, be those of the physicist; but there appears to be no reason to think that immaterial beings could not be subject to rigid laws. Again, there is, on the face of it, no reason to suppose that a being that cannot be seen or touched is likely to be more morally or religiously elevated, more worthy of respect, than one that can. The linking of the immaterial in that sense with the idea of 'spiritual' value stands in need of defence. If there is a difficulty in the idea that value is to be found in the normal world of stones, trees and human beings, it needs to be shown that exactly the same difficulty does not arise for the world which it is suggested is revealed to us by the paranormal.

But *is* there a difficulty in the idea that value is to be found in the world of extended, tangible, observable beings? Well, isn't this much true:

> The world as described by the natural scientist, and in particular by the physicist, is a world without value. We must, then, find gaps in the physicist's description if we are to leave any room for what is of value.

Now there may be nothing wrong with that thought in itself. To conclude, however, that we *must* turn to the paranormal if we are to find room for what is of value is to overlook the fact that 'finding a gap in another's description of a situation' can take a variety of forms. Consider a careful description of some great painting – for example, Leonardo da Vinci's *Madonna of the Rocks* – entirely in terms of the colour of paint at each point on the canvas; without, that is, any mention of what is *in* the painting. Most, I take it, will agree that this description leaves out the most important thing. Yet in its own terms it may contain no significant gap; there is no splash of red we can point to and say 'You didn't mention that'. We have, then, two quite different kinds of 'gap in a description' here. The kind of work needed to bring someone to see what his description leaves out will be quite different in the two cases. For example, a magnifying glass may be a help if someone has failed to mention a tiny patch of green in one corner, but is unlikely to be of much help to someone who simply cannot see the faces in the picture. (No doubt the latter deficiency is difficult to imagine in this case. We could think instead of a more abstract painting where for many there is a real difficulty in discerning the patterns.)

The parapsychologist I am speaking of insists that what is wrong with the claim that modern science gives us 'the fundamental truth about how things are' is the fact that the modern scientist systematically overlooks a certain kind of evidence. This parapsychologist does not question the claim (which no scientist need make) that what we might call 'the scientific method' is *the* method of determining the 'basic truth' about the world: that the world is that which is revealed to us by the most careful application of that method. Thus, he thinks that what we need is a bit of 'super-science' – an investigation into 'super-nature' – if we are to tell the whole story about the world; and, in particular, about people. Now the point of my analogy with a painting is that we can hold that current science does not tell us the whole truth about what a person is without suggesting that there is a gap in the scientist's account that needs to be filled by taking note of a further piece of evidence. We might add that there is at least room for the view that any change in my picture of the world that could be brought about in *that* way – that is, by a simple confrontation with some new empirical data – could not be a change that goes 'deep' in an ethical sense. A person who speaks of human beings as objects of a certain kind of respect is, it might be said, separated by an enormous gulf from one who speaks of us as, for example, 'complex stimulus–response systems'. The work needed to 'correct' the latter view must, therefore, be of a quite different order.

An analogy for this last point might be found in the relation between the views of three people on capital punishment. One defends capital punishment on the grounds that: 'It is an effective deterrent.' Another rejects it on the grounds that: 'It is not an effective deterrent.' A third rejects it on the grounds that: 'The taking of human life is an act of such horror that it can never be justified in terms of its effectiveness in promoting some social purpose.' For the third, the empirical evidence appealed to by the others is wholly irrelevant. Precisely because of that, we might say that he is separated from the other two by a much deeper gulf than that which separates them from each other.

I asked: Is there a difficulty in the idea that value is to be found in the world of extended, tangible, observable beings? One thing that stands in the way of clear thinking on this issue is the use we make of various contrasts: in particular, the 'material'/'immaterial' and 'body'/'mind' contrasts. Thus, the notion of the 'material' becomes connected in our thought with that of the 'materialistic' in the moral sense, with the idea of the world as described by the physicist, with the idea of what has mass, size and shape, with the idea of the observable, and perhaps others. The notion of the 'immaterial' is defined in our thought in terms of a contrast with that group of ideas. Powerful imagery helps to preserve such groupings of ideas in our minds. That which has no mass is free from the force of gravity and so is morally elevated. The body weighs us down, tying us to Earthly things: the pleasures of the flesh. Once one becomes aware of the role of this imagery, however, it should become clear that there is no reason to suppose that 'reality' carves up neatly along these lines. For example, the warm smile on her lips is, I take it, a feature of the world of extended, tangible, observable things. Does *it* figure in the physicist's description of the world? And what of the child's exclamation of joy on opening a birthday present, or the terror in the face of the man facing execution?

Examples of this kind will be of great importance to my argument in later stages of this book. Central to much of what I say will be the idea that a person is a *human being*: a being of flesh and blood, with a face and arms and legs. Now it might be thought that my use of the term 'human being' here is just a fudge. Have I not got to admit that the view that I am opposing to Descartes' is that people are simply their bodies: complex lumps of matter? The term 'human being', it might be said, disguises the unpalatable side of this in so far as in certain contexts it carries connotations of a more elevated kind: as when we say 'He is a real human being'.

Well, suppose it is said that Bach's music is 'just a lot of noise'. I will leave it to you to consider what is the correct response to *that* suggestion. Now compare that with the claim that people are 'simply bodies'. If that means 'You can see them, touch them, and weigh them' that is one thing. But if it means, for example, 'There is no difference between being interested in her and being interested in her body', where the latter phrase is tied up with lust or doctors, it is quite another. The term 'body' does, in certain contexts, allow one to slide too easily from one to the other. I use the term 'human being' in order to discourage moves of just this kind. Of course, if one thinks such moves are quite legitimate one will have worries about my use of the term 'human being'; but grounds for these worries do need to be established.

Developments in various sciences over the last hundred years have had an enormous impact on popular conceptions of the kind of beings that we are. It can, no doubt, be said that it is largely as a result of such developments that a great many people now have a picture of the person within which there is no room for the kind of value associated with talk of 'the soul'. My central point in this section has been that to hold (if one does) that this is a loss – that there is a serious deficiency in such pictures – is not yet to commit oneself to a particular view of the kind of work needed to correct the deficiency. Those who pursue an interest in the paranormal with the idea that this *must* be the key to the 'spiritual' would do well to remember that their activities might be viewed in the light of the following analogy. Confronted with a description of *The Madonna of the Rocks* in terms of colour patches, and the insistence that 'that is all there is to it', a man protests that several patches with subtle shades have been left out of the description. This man may know that something very important is missing from the description; but he is looking for what is missing in quite the wrong dimension.

Of course, this analogy might be totally unfair. It does, however, need to be shown that it is. It does, that is, need to be shown that we should be looking to the empirical sciences – whether of conventional or of less conventional forms – for answers to the most fundamental questions about ourselves and our relationship to the natural world. Much of this book will be an attempt to illustrate another form of argument that might be crucial to our questions here.

Further reading

Two books in which out-of-body experiences are appealed to in the way that I have been criticizing are Paul and Linda Badham, *Immortality or Extinction?* and David Lorimer, *Survival? Body, Mind and Death in the Light of Psychic Experience.* Such arguments are criticized in Antony Flew, *The Logic of Mortality,* chapter 10. The character of the relation between a 'scientific' and an 'everyday' picture of ourselves has an important place in Gilbert Ryle's thinking about these issues; see *The Concept of Mind,* and 'The World of Science and the Everyday World' in his *Dilemmas.*

3
Other Minds

1. The need for justification

John Stuart Mill writes:

> I conclude that other human beings have feelings like me, because, first, they have bodies like me, which I know, in my own case, to be the antecedent condition of feelings; and because, secondly, they exhibit the acts, and other outward signs, which in my own case I know by experience to be caused by feelings. I am conscious in myself of a series of facts connected by an uniform sequence, of which the beginning is modifications of my body, the middle is feelings, the end is outward demeanour. In the case of other human beings I have the evidence of my senses for the first and last links of the series, but not for the intermediate link. I find, however, that the sequence between the first and last is as regular and constant in those other cases as it is in mine. In my own case I know that the first link produces the last through the intermediate link, and could not produce it without. Experience, therefore, obliges me to conclude that there must be an intermediate link; which must either be the same in others as in myself, or a different one: I must either believe them to be alive, or to be automatons: and by believing them to be alive, that is, by supposing the link to be of the same nature as in the case of which I have experience, and which is in all other respects similar, I bring other human beings, as phenomena, under the same generalizations which I know by experience to be the true theory of my own existence. (Mill, 1889, pp. 243–4)

If this was intended as an explanation of how I ever come by the idea that there are people besides myself who have thoughts and sensations of the same kind as I do it would be pretty implausible. The young child, I take it, responds to others *as* people at a stage at which it would be quite absurd to suggest that he or she has gone through a reasoning process such as this. For example, she responds to a smile *as a smile* before we can reasonably suppose that she has noticed that when she herself smiles she is happy.

The suggestion is not, then, that this is how each of us first comes by the idea that there are people beside ourselves. That, it should be acknowledged, is to be explained in more fundamental, non-rational, terms. The suggestion is rather that each of us will, if we are concerned about the truth, demand a justification for that which we believe on instinct.

But why should it be supposed that there is any *special* need for justification here? Why should my belief that the world contains other people who feel pain, anger and so on be problematic in a way that my belief that the world contains trees is not? If I can justify the second belief by saying 'I have seen them' why should I not justify the first in the same way? (And if that justification won't do in either case why should the patching up needed in the one case be any different from that needed in the other?)

Well, many will, I think, feel that there is a crucial difference between these cases. The difference, it might be said, lies in the fact that I can never have *direct* knowledge of what another is feeling or thinking. I cannot actually *see* your anger or pain, as I can see the tree's branches waving in the wind. All that I actually *see* is the other's behaviour, and the judgement that another is angry or in pain always involves an interpretation of that behaviour. This becomes obvious when one reflects on the fact that a person can *pretend* to be angry or in pain: a person may behave as one who is angry or in pain, and yet not be in these states. That, it might be said, is sufficient to show that we must draw a sharp distinction between a person's *behaviour* and her mental states. Thus our judgements about another's mental states stand in need of some special form of justification in a way in which our judgements about the physical condition of a tree do not.

That line of thought both contributes to and is reinforced by the model of a person that emerges from Descartes' argument. The crucial feature of that model might be formulated in this way:

> All that we actually see when, as we normally say, we see another person is a physical body of a certain structure. What is crucial to there being a *person* there is something quite distinct from this. To

think that I am 'confronted with a person' is to think that causally connected with this lump of matter there is a non-material mind. It is here that thoughts, emotions, sensations and so on take place; and only the individual herself has direct access to this realm. Thus, the problem about how I can be justified in my belief that I am confronted with a person is distinct from, and additional to, any problem that there might be about how I can be justified in thinking that I am confronted with a material body of a certain form.

Mill's argument from analogy provides the further justification needed here.

We might, however, feel the need for something like the argument from analogy quite independently of such a philosophical model of a person. It is thought to be important that we should be able to *justify* the claim that some of the beings around us have a mental life. That thought might spring from a sense that it is important that we should be able to offer an argument to those whose views about *which* beings have a mental life are significantly different from our own. For example, there are those who question whether non-human animals, or at least certain species of them, have emotions and sensations. Now we might feel that it is important that we should be able to offer such people a *reason* for believing that they do: a reason for believing, for example, that the fish on the hook really does feel pain.

It is in this spirit that Peter Singer appeals to the argument from analogy in defence of the claim that non-human creatures feel pain:

> Do animals other than human beings feel pain? How do we know? Well, how do we know if anyone, human or non-human, feels pain? We know that we ourselves can feel pain. We know this from the direct experience of pain that we have when, for instance, somebody presses a lighted cigarette against the back of our hand. But how do we know that anyone else feels pain?

We know this, he suggests, through:

> ...an inference, but a perfectly reasonable one, based on observations of their behaviour in situations in which we would feel pain, and on the fact that we have every reason to assume that our friends are beings like us, with nervous systems like ours that can be assumed to function as ours do, and to produce similar feelings in similar circumstances.

Now we have exactly the same kind of reason to think that members of non-human species feel pain. For:

> Nearly all the external signs which lead us to infer pain in other humans can be seen in other species, especially the species most closely related to us – other species of mammals, and birds. ... In addition, we know that these animals have nervous systems very like ours, which respond physiologically as ours do when the animal is in circumstances in which we would feel pain. (Singer, 1978, pp. 10–11)

We might feel a similar need for the argument from analogy when confronted with an extreme form of racism.

2. *Which* bodily similarities are relevant?

But can the argument from analogy provide what we need here? I am supposed to conclude from the fact that I see other bodies like mine, which behave much as mine does, that behind these bodies lie other minds that have experiences similar to those of which I am immediately aware in my own case. Now a first thing to note here is that no other body, even within the human realm, is *exactly* like mine. So we need to ask: how similar, and in what respects, must another body be to mine if that similarity is to form a legitimate basis for this analogical reasoning?

It might be said that the answer to this question is obvious. It is quite clear that the *size* of the other body is pretty irrelevant, that its colour is completely irrelevant, that certain features of its structure – for example, those that distinguish the sexes – cast no doubt on whether the other body is relevantly like mine, and so on. On the other side, it might be said that it is quite obvious that other features of the structure – for example, what is inside its skull – are potentially of great relevance.

A first point to note about that is this. The core of the argument from analogy is an appeal to the fact that some of the bodies that I see around me are 'like mine'. *That* is what justifies me in believing that connected with these bodies are minds, which have experiences similar to my own. Now as soon as that is said there seems to be no avoiding the conclusion that the *more* like mine another body is the *better* is the justification that I have for my belief. Thus, *my* grounds for thinking that black women have a mental life like my own are less secure than are my grounds for thinking that white men do. And my grounds for thinking that dogs feel pain are considerably less secure than are my grounds for thinking that other human beings do. Now there will, no doubt, be argument there about just how great the bodily similarities are in the various different cases. My point at the moment is simply that Singer's use of the argument from analogy at this point is potentially disastrous. *If* we need the argument from analogy to justify our beliefs about the mental life of others then there is, it seems, room for legitimate disagreement in cases in which most of us would think there is no such room: room, for example, for legitimate disagreement about whether dogs feel pain.

Now it might be thought that the situation can be saved by an appeal to the idea that certain bodily similarities and differences are obviously relevant and others obviously irrelevant. But in what sense are the distinctions here 'obvious'? Well, this much can be said: attaching importance to certain similarities but not to others is something that comes naturally to us, or that we are drilled into. But we must remember that the whole point of the argument from analogy was to move us beyond a simple appeal to the fact that certain ways of thinking about and responding to others come naturally to us. It is supposed to show us that we are *justified* in ascribing a mental life to certain beings. If, then, it is to be worth anything at all it must show us that we are *justified* in regarding some bodily similarities and differences as relevant and others as irrelevant. But how is that to be done?

Suppose, for example, that we are confronted with the kind of case in which we might, in practice, feel a need for the argument from analogy: a case, say, in which someone seriously doubts whether dogs feel pain. It will be no use at this point appealing to the fact that it is 'just obvious' that it is quite irrelevant that dogs differ from us in having four legs and a tail, ears and noses up to six inches long, and so on. I am not denying that this *is* obvious: it is obvious to me at any rate, and I hope to you. My point is rather that it is obvious to me *because* it is obvious to me that dogs feel pain. One who, looking at a dog in (as I would say) obvious agony, seriously questions whether it is in pain, will also wonder whether number of legs, length of nose, and so on might not be relevant differences.

The general point here, then, is this. We need some kind of basis for picking out certain bodily features as relevant, and others as irrelevant, to the question of whether another has a mental life. One possible basis – that which I take it we appeal to in practice – will appeal to the fact that creatures that obviously feel pain have bodily features that we lack (for example, four legs) or lack bodily features that we have (for example, a human-shaped mouth); from which we conclude that these features are irrelevant to the question of whether they feel pain. But this is precisely the *reverse* of the relationship that is required by the argument from analogy! What that argument requires is this: someone who as yet has no views about which creatures, other than himself, have a mind, feel pain, and so on could be shown that certain bodily features are linked with such mental features, while others are not. But what, in my experience of *myself*, could show me this?

No doubt some will have ideas about how that question might be answered. I will briefly mention just one further consideration that might be introduced here. It is sometimes suggested that scientific knowledge of neurophysiology has a particularly central place in any serious effort to determine what sensations and so on should be ascribed to other species. Singer, for example, stresses the close similarities between the nervous systems of human and non-human species. Now one point to note here is that this appeal will only appear compelling to one who accepts that it is quite clear that *human beings* feel pain and so on. The research that establishes that certain features of the nervous system are closely linked with sensations such as pain only does so against the background of the assumption that at any rate the subjects of the physiological research are creatures that feel pain. While, then, this research might help to justify a step from 'Human beings feel pain' to 'Giant squids feel pain', it cannot help with the step from '*I* feel pain' to 'Other human beings feel pain'. For it to have any hope of justifying *that* step we would have to imagine someone performing complex neurophysiological experiments on *himself*. And while what would be required here may not be impossible in principle, in practice the results might be rather less useful than we would hope. For if someone starts off with the conviction that he is the only being with a mental life he need not concede that any experiment of this form provides him with any grounds for changing his view. If it seems obvious to him that the human being writhing in front of him is not a creature in pain, despite the fact that his neurophysiology has 'the relevant features', he will simply conclude that those features were not, on their own, quite the decisive mark of pain that his experience of his own case had led him to suppose. Perhaps what is crucial is the combination of that neurophysiology with a certain precise balance of chemicals in his stomach.

3. Facial expression and movements of facial flesh

We have been speaking of the crazy and corrupt. It might be objected that the fact that the argument from analogy will cut no ice with them does not show that it is not a perfectly valid argument: one that will, quite rightly, convince any sane and open-minded person that the human beings that he sees around him have a mental life like his own. But it must be remembered here that no 'sane and open-minded' person needs convincing of *that*. And my point has been that the apparent force of the argument depends on an illusion that is created by this fact. It is suggested that the person who really cares about the truth needs the argument from analogy in order to *justify* a belief that, no doubt, she already holds. But the argument provides no justification at all if it in any way *depends on* the very thing that it is supposed to establish. I have suggested that it does precisely this. For agreement about which physical features are relevant and which irrelevant is *dependent on* agreement about which other beings have minds and which do not.

I should perhaps stress at this point that I am not accusing Descartes, or Singer for that matter, of being either crazy or corrupt. Neither of them, I take it, ever seriously doubted in practice that other human beings have a mental life much like their own. (Though Descartes, it must be conceded, did say some rather odd things about animals – a point to which I will return.)

There is, I think, another, connected, illusion here. Consider another example. We are confronted with an extreme racist who insists that the black mother who grieves for her dead child does not really suffer as a white woman does. We might seek to convince the racist by some version of the argument from analogy. We point to the similarities in behaviour between the black woman and a white woman – perhaps including the racist with whom we are arguing – who has lost a child. Might not our racist, if she is prepared to give proper attention to what she observes, be forced to agree that there are no important differences between the two patterns of behaviour: no differences, that is, that could justify an ascription of different forms or degrees of suffering to the two women?

Let us focus on similarities in facial expression – which I take it will be central to any such argument. What *kind* of similarities will be relevant here? The point of this question might be brought out be considering the following cartoon faces. (See Figure 3.1.) We can ask: which pair of faces, a and b or c and d, are more similar to each other? The answer, I take it, is: that depends. The first pair of faces are clearly the more similar in terms of the expression on them. But the second are, perhaps, more similar in terms of patterns of ink on the page. Turning now to a pair of normal human faces we can say that there are (at

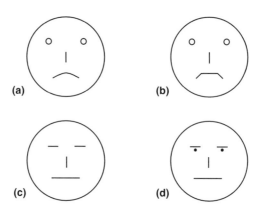

Figure 3.1

least) two different kinds of similarity in terms of which we could compare them. We could compare them in terms of the similarity or difference between the expressions on them: both are smiling, or both contemptuous, faces. Alternatively, we could compare them in terms of the similarity or difference between the arrangement and movement of the flesh that make them up.

We normally spontaneously respond to another face in the light of the *expression* on it. I respond to it *as* a smiling face; for example, I respond with a smile. If you later ask me what the face was like I might be able to offer a very fine-grained description in terms of the shade of emotion that was on it, and yet be able to say little about the arrangement of facial flesh in geometrical terms.

There is obviously a close relationship between the geometrical arrangement of facial flesh and the expression on the face. But the relationship is not of the following simple kind: if, and only if, the arrangement of flesh on two faces is very similar the expression on the faces is very similar. For, as the above cartoon faces bring out, a very small change in the arrangement of flesh can transform the expression on a face; and I take it that faces with large differences at the level of arrangements of flesh can be very similar in terms of the expression on them.

Similar points arise with other forms of behaviour. For example, I might recognize straight off that what I heard in her voice was contempt, and yet be quite incapable of describing what I heard in terms of modulation of tone and so on in such a way that another could work out from my description that there was contempt to be heard in the voice.

We will return in later chapters to other examples of this point. For the moment, I want simply to relate the above examples to our attempts to reason with the extreme racist. We point out to her, let us suppose, that the face of the grieving black woman is 'very similar' to that of the grieving white woman. But what *kind* of similarity is at issue here? If she is the racist I have in mind we can hardly expect her to accept, at the start, that the faces are very similar at the level of expression. For she simply doesn't see deep grief in the black woman's face. Indeed, that is precisely the problem with her. We can, then, hardly appeal to the 'obvious similarity' at this level as a first step in reasoning her out of her position.

If the starting point of our argument is to be a claim that we can expect her to accept despite her deep-seated racism, the similarity to which we appeal will, it seems, have to be at the level of arrangements of facial flesh. Will we find similarities of this kind between the faces of our two grieving women: similarities of a degree that might be sufficient to support an argument from analogy? I suppose that it depends on the case, and I have little idea how much we might reasonably hope for here. Let us imagine, however, that she does have to concede that there are close similarities of *this* kind between the two faces. Might she not reply that there is no reason to accept that similarities at *this* level provide any basis for the conclusion that the two women are undergoing similar emotional experiences? After all, it is not similarities and differences at *this* level that normally form the basis of our judgements about the emotions of others. We do not, in the normal course of things, regard the fact that two faces are very similar at *this* level as being reason for ascribing the same emotions to two people. Why, then, should our racist accept that such similarities carry the weight that we are trying to give them in this use of the argument from analogy?

4. Conclusion: justification and the mind/body divide

Descartes often reminds us that the human body – what we see or touch when we see or touch another living person – is, as he expresses it, 'corporeal substance' (Descartes, 1641, p. 185); it is, that is, something that can be adequately characterized in terms of its 'extension in length, breadth, and depth'. In the terms that I have used, he takes it to be clear, for example, that a proper description of a human face will be in terms of the geometrical arrangement and movement of the flesh of which it is composed. As we might also express this: a proper description of a human face – a description of what is actually to be seen *in* the face – will make no reference to the *expression* on it; no reference, for example, to the joy, pain or grief to be seen in it. For, Descartes will insist, that is not strictly speaking something that we *see*; it is something that we *infer* from what we see.

Now my point in this chapter might be expressed in this way. If we make this assumption then it seems unlikely that we will be able to justify anything remotely like our normal understanding of which beings have thoughts, emotions, sensations, and so on. For at the level of geometrical arrangements and movements of flesh we will not find the similarities in 'behaviour' that the argument from analogy needs. On the other hand, if we *don't* make this assumption then there seems to be no gap between 'behaviour' and 'the mental' of the kind that the argument from analogy is designed to bridge. For our descriptions of what we see of others will involve terms that do not leave open the question of whether they are beings of a kind that feel pain, grief and so on.

These points, it should be stressed, do not show that the radical mind/body split that is central to Descartes' dualism is a philosophical confusion. If the points are accepted, however, they do show that Descartes' position has some very uncomfortable implications. They give us reason, then, to seek alternative approaches to a philosophical understanding of the person.

Further reading

The most often quoted source of the argument from analogy is J.S. Mill, *An Examination of Sir William Hamilton's Philosophy*, 243–4. Peter Singer's use of the argument can be found in the first chapter of his *Animal Liberation*. Another version is presented in Stuart Hampshire, 'The Analogy of Feeling'. Hampshire offers a very different approach to these issues in 'Feeling and Expression'. A variety of responses to the argument from analogy are to be found in Norman Malcolm's 'Knowledge of Other Minds', P.F. Strawson, 'Persons' in his *Individuals*, D.C. Long, 'The Philosophical Concept of the Human Body', and Raimond Gaita, *Good and Evil* chapter 9. I have criticised the argument from analogy, along the general lines followed in this chapter, in 'Human Beings and Giant Squids'.

4
Mind and Behaviour

1. Cartesianism and contemporary views

Most contemporary English-speaking philosophers, and at least a substantial proportion of the wider reflective public, are deeply suspicious of the Cartesian understanding of a person. We might articulate something that is shared by the range of dominant contemporary views in this way: a person is an extended, tangible being that exists in the same world as tables, trees and mountains. But this formulation conceals differences that are every bit as important – some would say very much more important – than the similarities. We can, perhaps, best approach these modern developments by distinguishing a number of different strands in the Cartesian account.

First then, the Cartesian approach is marked by the central place given to the first person point of view. My knowledge of myself is, in Descartes' account, prior to my knowledge of the material world and prior to my knowledge of other people. It is through my experience of *myself* that I grasp what a person is; and through my experience of my own thoughts, emotions and sensations that I grasp what these are. To think of you as a person who has thoughts, emotions and sensations is to think of you as another being of the same kind as *I* am; a being that is subject to states of which I only have direct knowledge through my experience of them in my own case.

Second, the Cartesian approach insists that the real person is something other than the human being that we actually see when we 'meet another person'. Remember Descartes' phrase 'I (that is, my mind)'. The real person is 'the mind'. It is what goes on in this other entity – the mind – that explains the behaviour that we observe when we 'see another in pain' or when we 'see another fly into a rage'. That is to say, thought, emotion, sensation and so on are states or activities of this other entity: the mind. Descartes adds: the mind is a non-material thing that is causally connected with the brain.

We might add a third aspect of Descartes' view here. The extended, tangible thing – the 'human body' – that I see when I look at another human being is, in itself, a 'physical object': a physical object that is to be distinguished from other such objects simply in terms of its particular physical structure, and in terms of the fact that it is particularly closely causally connected with the mind. This feature of Descartes' view is reflected in his use of phrases such as 'the machine of the body' (Descartes, 1641, p. 195).

Now we can characterize contemporary accounts of the person in terms of their views about just *where* the fundamental defect in Cartesianism is to be found. From this point of view, we can distinguish two fundamentally different lines of criticism. The first takes as its central target the primacy that Descartes gives to the first person point of view. The second focuses on the thought that the mind is a non-material thing. In this chapter I want to consider the first of these lines of criticism. We will turn to the second in the following chapter.

2. The social character of our mental vocabulary

We have already explored one difficulty in which Descartes may be implicated by the kind of priority he gives to his experience of *himself*: if we understand the relation between my thought of myself and my thought of others in the terms suggested by Descartes' argument we are committed to the idea that I need some special justification for thinking that there *are* any other beings with a mental life like my own – and it is not at all clear that that can be provided (see Chapter 3). Now, an alternative understanding of the notion of a person builds on this criticism, suggesting that Descartes' whole approach involves a quite wrong picture of the kind of meaning possessed by our talk about thoughts, emotions, sensations and so on. The meaning of that talk is not to be found in some association each of us makes between the word 'pain' or the word 'anger' and an 'inner' state: an inner state to which each of us has immediate access only in our own case. For the meaning of the word 'anger', for example, cannot be separated from the particular patterns of behaviour in which anger is characteristically manifested.

To see the force of this suggestion one needs to start, not where Descartes starts, but with the fact that a word such as 'anger' is a word in a public language: a word in a language that I share with others; and, with that, a word that has its primary role in discourse with others about my own, or another's, emotional state. Now when we approach the matter from this perspective one of the first things that should strike us is the fact that the use of the word 'anger' is closely bound up with the behaviour in which anger is characteristically expressed. One aspect of this is seen in the way in which the other's behaviour plays a central role in my readiness to judge that he or she is angry. It is what I see in Mary's behaviour, and in particular, perhaps, what I see in her face, that leads me to think that she is angry. With that, I might justify my claim that 'Mary is angry' by pointing to the look on her face when John walked in, her sharp tone of voice, the fierce way in which she threw down the suitcases, and so on. Again, I might justify my claim that John appreciates the significance of his opponent's last move by pointing to his worried expression and to the fact that he moves his bishop in front of his queen. Now certainly I do not base *all* of my judgements about mental states on my observation of someone's behaviour. In particular, I do not, the Cartesian will be quick to insist, base my judgement that *I* am angry on my observation of my own behaviour. But we will return to that. For the moment we need simply note that from the *social* perspective that we are now adopting we will think of such cases as simply one – albeit an important one – among others. We will not, as the Cartesian approach does, focus on such cases as being *the* central examples of judging someone to be angry or judging that someone understands.

Another important face of the link between our understanding of what 'anger' is and the behaviour in which anger is characteristically expressed is seen in the *significance* that the information that someone is 'angry' may have for us. When I learn that someone is angry I learn things such as the following: if I want to avoid a nasty confrontation it would be a good idea to keep out of his way for a while, a good idea not to raise that touchy subject that we need to discuss sometime, and so on. These are significant aspects of the kind of importance that the notion of 'anger' has in our lives. Similarly, just as we see that someone 'understands' a certain problem in the construction of a house through observing the way in which he proceeds with the work, so a central feature of the *importance* of the information that he 'understands' lies in the fact that if he understands the problem he can be expected to take measures that will overcome it. Again, just as we learn that another has a pain in her foot by seeing her limp, wince and so on, so the significance of the fact that she has a pain in her foot lies in part in the fact that, for example, she would never make it to the cinema if she had to walk.

Some philosophers who have reflected on points like this have toyed with the idea that we might '*analyse*' talk about mental states in terms of talk about behaviour. Thus, it might be suggested, very crudely, that: to say that someone is angry is just to say that she is *behaving* in ways that are characteristic of anger. Or that: pain just *is* crying out, writhing on the ground, and so on. Suggestions of this general form are known as 'behaviourism'. Such suggestions at least have the virtue of not leaving us with the 'problem of other minds' that was discussed in Chapter 3. But there are very obvious objections to any proposal that is quite as crude as these. For one thing, it seems clear that someone can be angry or in pain without this being manifested in her behaviour. For another, it seems clear that, in many cases at least, an individual's judgements about her *own* mental states are not based on observation of her own behaviour. For a third, it seems clear that the *significance* for us of the fact that someone is in a certain mental state is not exhaustively described in terms of the behaviour that we can expect from her. The significance that a severe pain in my foot has for *me* has little to do with the kind of behaviour that can be expected from me. Equally, that another has a severe pain in her foot is not simply a reason for thinking that she won't make it to the cinema on foot; it is also a reason for feeling sorry for her and trying to help her.

Those who are sympathetic to the idea that we might, in some sense, '*analyse*' talk about mental states in terms of talk about behaviour have been aware of objections like these, and so have proposed forms of analysis that are much more carefully worked out than the simple versions outlined above. It is suggested, for example, that: to say that someone is angry is to say that he is *disposed* to behave in ways that are characteristic of anger. Or that: to say that someone is angry is to say that he *would* behave in characteristically angry ways if certain circumstances arose. We need not, however, dwell on these, often very sophisticated, proposals; for there is, on the face of it, no reason to assume that any analysis of talk about mental states in terms of talk about something else should be possible. To assume that it is is to assume that it must be possible to say everything that we now say about a person's emotions, sensations, and so on in a terminology from which all mental state terms have been eliminated. And there appears to be no reason to make such an assumption.

But however that may be, my purpose in drawing attention to these links between our talk about mental states, on the one hand, and human behaviour on the other, has not been to suggest that we should be looking for some such analysis. My point has rather been this. We might take as our starting point, not the solitary individual, shut away from the world, and keeping a record of his or her own mental states; but rather the social world in which people judge that each other understand something, are in pain, are angry, or are in love, and in which these judgements have various forms of significance: forms that are, in many cases, closely linked with the behaviour in which such states are characteristically expressed. Now it is true that – once he has dug himself out of his general sceptical doubt – Descartes can, in a sense, acknowledge these facts about our social relations. But from the perspective of his philosophy, these appear as secondary facts. For Descartes, we should look to the case in which a person says of *himself* 'I am thinking', 'I am angry' or 'I am in pain' if we want to see the most straightforward case in which a person forms a judgement about someone's mental state. Cases in which someone judges that *another* is in pain or is angry are to be fitted in afterwards as best they can (which, as we have seen, may not be very well).

The difference between the perspectives can perhaps be clarified by considering an imaginary case. Suppose that we encounter someone who says 'I am in pain' or 'I am angry' when he is in pain or angry, but has *no* idea how to tell on the basis of what he sees in another whether that person is in pain or is angry; and, with that, *no* idea what to expect from another who, he has been told, is in pain or angry. From Descartes' perspective, there would, in such a case, be no reason to say that this person does not understand the words 'pain' and 'anger' just as we do. It is just that he has failed to notice that there is a connection between pain and certain patterns of behaviour, between anger and certain patterns of behaviour, and so on – much as someone might have a completely adequate understanding of the word 'green' and yet not be aware that green objects reflect light of a certain wavelength. By contrast, from the social perspective of which I have been speaking that way of putting the matter will not seem to capture the depth of the difference between this individual and ourselves. Such a person would be separated from the rest of us in a much more radical way than is suggested by the analogy with the word 'green'. While we will, no doubt, agree that there are grounds for saying that he has *some* understanding of the words 'pain' and 'anger', there are also substantial grounds for saying that his understanding is far from complete. For his use of these words is severely restricted, and in a way such that he is going to be at sea with the simplest conversations about these states.

When we say 'You can't make him walk; he has a terrible pain in his foot' he simply does not see the connection between the two halves of our remark; and similarly when we say 'Don't expect too much cheerful chat from him for a while; he is in a frightful rage' or 'He would make a hopeless dog trainer; he is terrified of dogs'.

I have not offered an argument for the claim that, in our philosophical thinking about people and their mental states, we *ought* to give priority to the social perspective, as opposed to the individual, first person perspective of Cartesianism. My hope is that once the options are clearly presented there will be few left who need convincing. But there are further obstacles to a wholehearted acceptance of the social perspective, and these need to be explored.

3. Private language (i)

Part of the attraction of Descartes' approach to the question of what a person is is closely bound up with the special place that he gives to the first person point of view. Perhaps it leads to problems concerning how each of us could know anything about the mental life of others. But is there not *something* right in the thought that each of us can know his or her own mental states with a kind of immediacy and certainty that is denied to others? And if there is something right in that, then it is an important truth: one that we must somehow capture in our account of what a person is.

A first point to note here is that this 'truth' – such as it is – may not be quite as general as Descartes supposed it to be. He writes:

> By the word thought, I understand all that which so takes place in us that we ourselves are immediately conscious of it; and, accordingly, not only to understand, to will, to imagine, but even to perceive, are here the same as to think. (Descartes, 1641, p. 167)

In what sense am I 'immediately conscious' of my own understanding? Well, this much I take it is clear: I may *think* that I understand a certain argument or a certain person and yet be quite wrong. Indeed, others may see long before I do that I do not really understand what is going on.

Consider some other examples, not this time from Descartes' list. Love and anger are, I take it, mental states. Do I inevitably know of these states in myself with an immediacy and certainty that is denied to others? Is it not a quite familiar feature of our experience that others should see before John does that he is falling in love with Mary? On the other side, are we not often quite ready to say of someone that while she thinks that she is in love she is not really? Again, is it not quite possible for me to fail to notice until it is pointed out to me by another that I was really quite angry about what someone said?

Well, there may be room for argument about those examples. But rather than pursue that I want to focus on a category of mental state in connection with which Descartes' suggestion *does* seem to hold. For example, I cannot, it seems, fail to recognize that I have a sharp pain in my toe; and if it seems to me that I have a sharp pain in my toe then I certainly do. By contrast (provided that the pain is not *too* sharp, and I have reasonable self-control) others may remain completely ignorant of what I am undergoing. (If you want to protest that a pain in the toe is not a *mental* state but a *physical* one, go ahead and protest! I believe that this feature of the way in which we describe such cases is of considerable significance. But that is a point to which we will return later.)

Now it is, it might be said, one of the great virtues of the Cartesian picture that it makes sense of this obvious fact. For according to that picture pain is an inner state, quite distinct from any of its outward manifestations. I learn what pain is through my experience of my own pains. And when I judge that I am in pain, I am not making a judgement about how I am *behaving*. I am making the judgement that this – what I am now feeling – is of the same kind as that which I labelled 'pain' in the past. Since only the individual herself can directly inspect the sensation that she feels, only she is in the ideal position to classify what she is feeling as a 'pain'. With that, the directness of the confrontation ensures that there is, for her, even less room for the possibility of a mistake about what she is feeling than there is in a case in which I judge that a vase right in front of me in broad daylight is 'blue'.

What should we make of this proposal? Here is Wittgenstein's comment:

> If he now said, for example: 'Oh, I know what "pain" means; what I don't know is whether *this*, that I have now, is pain' – we should merely shake our heads and be forced to regard his words as a queer reaction which we have no idea what to do with. ... That expression of doubt has no place in the language-game; but if we cut out human behaviour, which is the expression of sensation, it looks as if I might *legitimately* begin to doubt afresh. (Wittgenstein, 1968, §288)

This is, for a number of reasons, a difficult passage. One of the things that makes it difficult is the fact that, while it might seem that some of what Wittgenstein says supports the Cartesian view, his aim is to point to a fundamental *objection* to that view. The objection might be expressed by saying that the Cartesian view does not go far enough. What, at best, the Cartesian picture of my relation to my own sensations would explain is this: it is extremely unlikely that anyone should take what she is feeling to be a 'pain' when it is not; and, with that, there is very little room for an individual to doubt whether what she is feeling is pain. As I expressed it: there is, for her, even less room for the possibility of a mistake about what she is feeling than there is in a case in which I judge that a vase right in front of me in broad daylight is 'blue'. But *that*, Wittgenstein suggests, is not what needs to be explained. What we need to make philosophical sense of is the fact that 'the expression of doubt has no-place in the language-game'; that is to say, it *makes no sense* to suppose that while there is nothing wrong with someone's grasp of the meaning of the word 'pain' he makes a mistake about whether what he is feeling is pain. Now on the Cartesian picture as I have presented it this supposition would certainly *make sense*. It would, at best, just be very unlikely that it should happen. For, as I expressed the matter, when I report that I am in pain I am making the judgement that this – what I am now feeling – is of the same kind as that which I labelled 'pain' in the past. And since, of course, it *makes sense* to suppose that I have misremembered what I labelled 'pain' in the past, it *makes sense* to suppose that I am mistaken in my judgement that what I am now feeling is of the same kind as what I have, in the past, called 'pain'.

The point is, perhaps, worth repeating in slightly different terms. On the Cartesian picture, what is crucial for the truth of my judgement that what I am feeling is correctly classified as 'pain' is this: the sensation that I am feeling now is of the same kind as those I have previously classified as 'pain'. Now what grounds do I have for believing that *that* is so? The only possible answer seems to be: my memory of what I have classified as 'pain' in the past. Now this dependence on memory seems to create a space for doubt or mistake in just the sense that the Cartesian picture sought to exclude. Confronted with the question 'How do you know that your memory impression of the sensation that you called "pain" last week is not confused?' the only possible answer seems to be: 'It doesn't seem confused to me'. Which is just to say: 'That really *is* my memory impression'. Wittgenstein compares this with a case in which someone buys 'several copies of the morning paper to assure himself that what it said was true' (Wittgenstein, 1968, §265).

The crucial issue is not, I should stress, that the Cartesian picture leaves *significant* room for doubt or mistake about whether what I am feeling is a 'pain', but that it leaves room for it at all. Wittgenstein's point is that, in our normal employment of it, the word 'pain' is used in such a way that the idea that I might have mistaken my own pain for something else simply makes no sense. In this sense, we might say, the Cartesian picture is not sufficiently radical.

In the passage quoted above, Wittgenstein locates the source of this difficulty in the way in which the Cartesian has 'cut out human behaviour, which is the expression of sensation'. To appreciate the force of his suggestion we must note first that, in practice, someone says 'That hurts!' in the sorts of circumstance in which she pulls her hand back sharply and rubs it, she lets out a cry and her face contorts, and so on. Of course, we often find behaviour of the latter, non-verbal, kind without the verbal behaviour: without the cry 'That hurts!' In particular, we find this with animals and very young children. Conversely, people sometimes say 'That hurts' or 'I have a pain in my foot' while showing none of the familiar non-verbal manifestations of pain. For all that, we do, in practice, judge that someone – say a child who is learning to talk – has grasped the meaning of the word 'pain', or of the expression 'That hurts', by noticing how her use of these words fits into the rest of her behaviour. It is in circumstances in which she has just burned her hand and she is clutching it and crying that we teach her to say 'It hurts'. And we judge that she is using these words correctly provided that her words 'That hurts' or 'I have a pain in my foot' generally fit in with her circumstances – she has just been burned – and her non-verbal behaviour in the standard ways.

According to the Cartesian picture, this method of teaching the meaning of the word, and of judging that another means by the word what we do, is indirect. Only the person herself can know *directly* what she means by the word 'pain'. For, as we might express it, the word 'pain' is defined in terms of the felt quality of an experience to which only the individual herself has direct access. Now, as we saw in Chapter 3, this creates serious problems for the question: can the individual ever have grounds for thinking that when the words 'I am in pain' issue from another's lips there is another person suffering what I would call 'pain'? But Wittgenstein's point goes deeper in that it attacks the Cartesian picture at just the point that seems to be its greatest strength. For it brings out that this picture allows the *possibility* of doubt and mistake in the case in which the individual is inclined to say of *herself* 'I am in pain'.

4. Private language (ii)

But how does Wittgenstein's emphasis on the way in which self-ascriptions of 'pain' are linked with other, non-verbal, expressions of pain, such as moaning and limping, remove this possibility; and so achieve what the Cartesian picture tries, but fails, to achieve? To answer this question we must take note of another aspect of Wittgenstein's approach to this link. He writes:

> [H]ow does a human being learn the meaning of the names of sensations?—of the word 'pain' for example. Here is one possibility: words are connected with the primitive, the natural, expressions of the sensation and used in their place. A child has hurt himself and he cries; and then adults talk to him and teach him exclamations and, later, sentences. They teach the child new pain-behaviour. (Wittgenstein, 1968, §244)

I take the central message of this passage to be that if we want to understand the place in our lives of words such as 'That hurts!' we should compare them to a spontaneous cry of pain. When a person says 'That hurts!' or 'I have a pain in my foot' what she is doing is, in a certain respect, akin to what someone does when she cries out in pain.

But in *what* respect is it akin to this? It will be helpful here to make another comparison. Consider a case in which someone suffers a severe burn: she lets out a cry, her face contorts, and she draws her hand back sharply. Compare this with a case in which someone rounds a corner and finds herself face to face with something that looks very like a tiger: she lets out a cry, turns white as a sheet, and turns and runs. In the second case there is room for the thought: 'That isn't really a tiger; she only thinks it is, and that is why she reacts as she does.' Is there room for an analogous thought in the first case? Well, on the face of it there is clearly at least one sense in which there is not. At any rate, the *Cartesian* will certainly not want to leave room for the suggestion that: 'She only thinks she is in pain; and that is why she reacts as she does.' For one of the driving forces behind the Cartesian approach is the idea that we cannot be mistaken about whether we ourselves are, for example, in pain. But further, there seems to be nothing to be said for the suggestion that the response of crying out, and so on is mediated by thought – as it might be said that the response to the tiger in the second case is mediated by thought. Everyone ought to agree that (at least in standard cases) no *judgement* is involved here: there is no question of comparing what I am feeling now with sensations I have felt in the past, deciding on the basis of this comparison that what I am feeling is pain, and so concluding that the appropriate response is to cry out, and so on.

Are we to say of *this* case that the person could not be making a mistake about what she feels? Well, if we do say that, we should not take this to mean: her judgement that she is in pain is certainly correct. For it is seriously misleading to suggest that the person makes any such judgement. What we *can* say – at least on Wittgenstein's account – is that if there is no insincerity – no attempt at deception – in her response then there is no room for the thought that: 'Perhaps her behaviour is not a reliable guide to her state. Perhaps she is not really in pain.' *That* is the sense in which she 'could not be making a mistake.' (Notice that the words 'if there is no insincerity – no attempt at deception – in her response' do *not* slip in qualifications that take us back to the Cartesian view. For on the Cartesian view there is room for the thought that: the way in which her pains *naturally* find expression in her behaviour is very different from that in which mine do. There is, that is, room for a doubt about whether another who is crying out, and so on, is really in pain without there being any suggestion that the other is, for example, putting on a show.)

Consider now another case, exactly the same as the above apart from the fact that this time the person cries 'God, that hurts!' Are we to say of this case: her judgement that it hurts – that she is in pain – is certainly correct? Well, if there was something misleading in the previous case in saying that she makes such a judgement perhaps there is something equally odd in this case. Perhaps we can say that her cry 'That hurts!' is related to her pain in something like the way in which her groans and contorted face are. Of course, the relation is not *exactly* the same. For one thing, the verbal expression of pain is not a 'natural' expression in the sense that a cry or contorted face is; for there is, I take it, a straightforward sense in which the former, but not the latter, is learned. No doubt connected with this is the fact that it may, in the case of a significant pain, take a conscious effort to *inhibit* the non-verbal expressions of pain; where, by contrast, something more like a conscious decision is involved in *expressing* one's pain verbally. But that – which is, perhaps, in any case a difference of degree – is irrelevant to the connection that Wittgenstein wishes to make between the two. For his point is this: just as with the non-verbal expression there is no question of 'comparing what I am feeling now with what I felt last week to see if it is close enough for me to cry out in just the same way', so, at least in standard cases, there is with *verbal* expressions of pain no question of 'comparing what I am feeling now with what I felt last week to see if it is close enough for me to utter the words "That hurts!"' 'Comparing' doesn't come into it. And it is only because it doesn't that we can say: if there is no insincerity – no attempt at deception – in her verbal response then there is no room for the thought that: 'Perhaps her words are not a reliable guide to her state; perhaps she is not really in pain.' *That* is the sense in which she 'could not be making a mistake'.

The point might be made in the following way. In practice, we say that someone has mastered the use of the words 'I am in pain', 'My foot hurts' and so on, when such self-ascriptions fit in with the rest of his behaviour in appropriate ways. Suppose that someone – a young child, say – regularly said things like 'I have a terrible pain in my foot' when he had not suffered any physical injury, and none of the rest of his behaviour fitted in, in at all the right way, with the suggestion that he had a terrible pain in his foot: he does not limp, rub his foot, his face shows none of the characteristic marks of pain, and so on. We would not, I take it, in practice say of such a case that: 'A person cannot be mistaken about whether or not he is in pain; so in pain he is.' One who drew that conclusion would have misunderstood the force of the suggestion that 'a person cannot be mistaken about whether or not he is in pain'. It is, I take it, clear that in such a case we would, as we would put it, 'correct the child's English'. We would tell him that he has got the wrong word. We would only allow that he has mastered the English words 'pain', 'hurt', and so on in so far as his self-ascriptions fit in with the rest of his behaviour in appropriate ways. This, it should be stressed, is quite a flexible business. For example, a person will sometimes say 'I have a pain in my finger' while showing no non-verbal signs of pain. She may write in a letter 'My leg doesn't hurt any more' when it is clear from her face and the way that she walks that she is still in serious pain. Neither of these need cast any doubt on her grasp of word 'pain' or 'hurt' provided that they have as a background a rich range of cases in which what she says about herself fits in with her other behavioural expressions of pain. But that background is crucial. For it is only against such a background that it can be said that: 'If she is sincerely inclined to say of herself that she is, as she puts it, "in pain" then she certainly is in pain.'

The idea that 'A person cannot be mistaken about whether or not he is in pain' has the sense that it does, and only *could* have sense, within the context of the close link, stressed by Wittgenstein, between pain and its public expression in behaviour.

5. Knowledge of others

A central concern of this chapter has been the relationship between the individual's knowledge of her *own* mental states and her knowledge of the mental states of *others*. Closely linked with that has been a concern about the relationship between our judgements about a person's mental states and our observation of the forms of behaviour in which mental states are manifested. I suggested in the opening section of Chapter 3 that the philosophical idea that there is some special problem about our knowledge of the mental life of others – that being the problem to which the argument from analogy is a response – may have its roots in the following thought:

> I can never have *direct* knowledge of what another is feeling or thinking. I cannot actually *see* your anger or pain, as I can see the tree's branches waving in the wind. All that I actually *see* is the other's behaviour, and the judgement that another is angry or in pain always involves an interpretation of that behaviour. This becomes obvious when one reflects on the fact that a person can *pretend* to be angry or in pain: a person may behave as one who is angry or in pain, and yet not be in these states. That … is sufficient to show that we must draw a sharp distinction between a person's *behaviour* and her mental state. Thus our judgements about another's mental states stand in need of some special form of justification in a way in which our judgements about the physical condition of a tree do not.

Now I do not for one second wish to deny that our attempts to get clear about what another is feeling or thinking face special problems: problems of a kind that do not arise for other forms of judgement. I *do* wish to deny, however, that the above statement offers an accurate characterisation of what those problems are.

Consider, first, the place that the idea of *pretence* has in the above reasoning. It is, in effect, concluded from the fact that a person can pretend to be angry that we can never *see* that a person is angry – as we can *see* that this is a tree. And so my judgement that another is angry always requires an inference from what I do see – namely his behaviour – to an 'underlying' mental state: an inference of the form provided by the argument from analogy. But the matter does not have to be understood in that way. One who thinks we need an argument from analogy thinks that when I see someone fall to the ground, clutch his head and groan immediately after he has been struck on the head by a brick I need some *justification* for taking him to be in pain. That the other is behaving in this way is never *in itself* any reason at all for thinking that he is in pain; for according to the dualist I need a reason for thinking that this kind of behaviour is a sign of pain. Now I have been suggesting that the reverse of this is true. When we see someone behaving in such a way we need some justification for *doubting* that he is in pain. There is an onus on one who expresses doubt to produce grounds for doubt: grounds, for example, for thinking that the person is putting on a show. Sometimes such a doubt will be in place. But equally, it will often be simply idiotic. If someone seriously suggests that my two-year-old child who has hit his thumb with a hammer might just be pretending to be in pain I will not take him seriously. And if someone – a philosopher perhaps – suggests that I *should* take him seriously, he is going to have to produce an argument for this claim.

The difficulty involved in getting to know another is not, as the dualist picture implies, the fact that we can never 'confirm directly' how another's mental states predispose him to act. It is not that there is some completely general obstacle to 'direct knowledge' of another's feelings or thoughts, or that we can never simply see that another is angry or thinks there is someone at the door. The difficulty is, in part, simply that human life is pretty complicated. A person's state at any moment is a complex pattern that lies at the intersection of many forces. He is not just in pain. He is also slightly irritated by the man on his right, trying to impress the woman on his left, worried about his overdraft, depressed about his work, and much more besides. In so far as his behaviour is unambiguously expressive of one aspect of his present state it inevitably obscures others. Now in practice it can, of course, be extremely difficult to sort out the tangle. But we should not let our desire properly to acknowledge that difficulty tempt us back into the dualist fold. For the difficulty is quite different from that presented by the dualist. This emerges in part in the fact that it can be as difficult – in some cases it is very much *more* difficult – for the individual himself to sort out the tangle as it is for another to do so. It emerges too in the steps that we may take in an effort to surmount the difficulty. We might, for example, remove the man on his right and (especially!) the woman on his left, thus enlarging the possibilities of an anxiety or depression finding a purer expression in his behaviour, speech and manner. Steps of this form are quite irrelevant to the 'problem of our knowledge of others' that is central to the Cartesian image.

Brief mention should be made of two other dimensions of difficulty that are relevant here. First, people are reticent to expose themselves to others; and the reticence runs deep in a way such that, even when someone wants to be completely open with another, she may find it extremely difficult to articulate her thoughts and feelings at all adequately. Second, there are, on the other side, a great variety of pressures in each of us that militate against a proper acknowledgement of the thoughts and feelings of others: pressures that include, for example, mere callous indifference, lack of imagination, and the fear of acknowledging the force of another's anger or the depth of her suffering.

One of the dangers of dualist imagery is that its simple picture of the obstacle to proper knowledge of another may blind us to the character of the real difficulties that we may need to overcome there.

6. The joy in another's face

I have been speaking of the relationship between 'mind' and 'behaviour': the relationship between, for example, the idea that someone is angry and the fact that he is red in the face, shouting, and storming around the room. And I have suggested that certain confusions concerning the kind of meaning possessed by our mental vocabulary are involved in a familiar picture of that relationship. In this section I want to approach the matter from, so to speak, the other end: suggesting that confusions about the idea of 'behaviour' play an equally important, and damaging, role in philosophical discussions of these issues.

In Chapter 3, section 3 I contrasted a description of a face in terms of the expression on it with a description of the same face in terms of geometrical arrangements of flesh. I tried to bring out the contrast by appealing to the idea of similarities and differences between cartoon faces. And I suggested that the same contrast had application to other forms of behaviour. Consider, for example, the following descriptions of human behaviour: 'He opened the window and smiled at the woman outside', 'He checkmated her in five moves', 'He danced a highland fling', 'He glared at her with a scowl on his face', 'She said that it was time to go' 'He got divorced' 'Her face lit up with joy'. These everyday descriptions of human behaviour are of a quite different form from descriptions in terms of movements of matter: 'The fingers of his right hand converged on the piece of wood, and the whole hand moved north-east at 3 m.p.h.', or whatever. We might say that in some sense they are descriptions of 'the same thing'; just as we might say that we can describe a single thing – a painting – in terms of splodges of paint on a canvas or in terms of what it is a painting of. But the *meanings* of the two descriptions are quite different: there is no possibility of translating the one form of description into the other. One way in which this comes out is this. A range of quite different movements of matter is consistent with a given description of action or expression: for example, when I learn that 'He divorced his wife' or that 'He voted for the motion' I learn little about how his body moved. The other side of this is that a description of how his body moved may not tell me much about what action he performed: this particular movement of hands in the absence of a chess board, or when the pieces were arranged differently, would not be a checkmating.

When thinking philosophically, we may be tempted by the idea that what we really *see* when we look at another is simply matter in motion: that a *strict* description of what is seen would be a description in terms of the 'language of physics'. While we may be slightly hazy (as I certainly am!) just what the language of current physics is, we feel clear that a strict description of what we actually *see* would be one that leaves completely open all questions about the person's 'mental state'. On this view, we should say, for example, not 'He said that it was time to go', but 'The sounds "It is time to go" came from his mouth'; for the former description presupposes views about what he *meant* in producing these sounds. We should say, not 'Her face lit up with joy', but 'The corners of her mouth rose by 0.35 cm … '; for the former description, quite illegitimately on this view, imports the mental term 'joy' into a description of the behaviour.

And so the question arises: what justification do we ever have for moving from what we actually see to conclusions about the other's mental states?

Our normal, everyday, descriptions of the behaviour of others leave no room for that quite general gap between 'descriptions of behaviour' and 'descriptions of mental states'. But can our normal descriptions be taken at face value? (And, incidentally, what is '*face* value'?!) Do I really *see* joy in the other's face, or hear the anger in his voice? Certainly we talk in these ways. But are not these ways of speaking elliptical? Must we not agree that what I actually *see* is simply certain movements of facial flesh that I *interpret* as an expression of joy?

Consider an analogy. On a piece of paper there is a pattern of dots in which I clearly 'see' a house. Do I really *see* the house, or do I merely see the dots, which I then interpret as being a picture of a house? Well, someone might see the dots and yet not see the house. (I am assuming that the picture is not so clear that the house immediately hits everyone in the face.) It does not follow that the one who 'sees' the house is not really *seeing* the house: that he really only sees the dots, which he then *interprets* as being a picture of a house. Indeed, it is clear, I think, that that description will not do. For we can imagine someone who interprets this as a picture of a house, but simply cannot see it in that way. Perhaps he has been reliably informed that this artist always does houses like that; and so, if asked, he will say with complete confidence that it is a picture of a house. Yet, for the life of him, he cannot *see* a house in the dots.

If you are not clear what I mean by the phrase 'see a house in the dots' consider the following drawing. (See Figure 4.1) What do you see: a duck or a rabbit? *Both* are there to be seen in the picture. But at any one time one only *sees* one of them. (Wittgenstein has a fascinating discussion of issues raised by this example. See his *Philosophical Investigations*, Part II section xi.)

The point of this digression about houses, ducks and rabbits has simply been to raise a doubt about the insistence that we do not, strictly speaking, *see* the joy in another's face, the anger in another's eyes, and so on: that we do not, strictly speaking, *see* people laughing at jokes or writhing in agony. We were asked to agree that whenever our description of another involves terms that 'imply mentality', we are going beyond a pure description of what we see: going beyond a pure description of her behaviour. It is suggested that in all such cases we are placing an interpretation on, or drawing an inference from, what we actually see. But not only do we not *have* to describe the matter in that way; on the face of it such descriptions of the situation are simply wrong. For example, we can imagine someone interpreting another's

Figure 4.1

look as being one of anger, or inferring from the other's look that he is angry, and yet not, for the life of her, being able to see the anger in the other's look. As with the dots and the house, her interpretation is grounded in her prior knowledge that this is the (perhaps rather eccentric) way in which *his* anger finds expression.

We can, perhaps, imagine a more radical case than this: a case of someone who, to adopt a term of Wittgenstein's, is aspect blind in this area. The following extract from a paper by Oliver Sacks, in which he discusses the condition of an autistic woman, may give some feeling for what a more radical case could be like:

> I was struck by the enormous difference, the gulf, between Temple's immediate, intuitive recognition of animal moods and signs and her extraordinary difficulties understanding human beings, their codes and signals, the way they conduct themselves. One cannot say that she is devoid of feeling or has a fundamental lack of sympathy. On the contrary, her sense of animals' moods and feelings is so strong that these almost take possession of her, overwhelm her at times. She feels she can have sympathy for what is physical or physiological – for an animal's pain or terror – but lacks empathy for people's states of mind and perspectives. When she was younger, she was hardly able to interpret even the simplest expressions of emotion; she learned to 'decode' them later... Temple had longed for friends at school and would have been totally, fiercely loyal to a friend (for two or three years, she had an imaginary friend), but there was something about the way she talked, the way she acted, that seemed to alienate others... Something was going on between the other kids, something swift, subtle, constantly changing – an exchange of meanings, a negotiation, a swiftness of understanding so remarkable that sometimes she wondered if they were all telepathic. She is now aware of the existence of these social signals. She can infer them, she says, but she herself cannot perceive them, cannot participate in this magical communication directly... (Sacks, 1995, pp. 256–60)

This is a striking passage – as is Sacks' whole discussion of this woman's life. While I am far from clear just how her condition should be described, we can, perhaps, safely say that she does not see the *expression* in the faces and behaviour of other human beings. (As we can imagine someone who, try as he might, cannot see the rabbit in the duck–rabbit figure.) She can 'infer' from what she does see that the other is afraid, angry or friendly; but she cannot, as we can, 'perceive' the fear, anger or friendliness in the other's features.

It may not be easy to say what exactly that contrast amounts to. (I will say something about this in Chapter 7, section 3.) But we must not let any difficulties we have with that stand in the way of an acknowledgement of a serious distortion in certain philosophical models of our relation to others. One might say that according to these models the *real* world is the world as it is experienced by one with autism. That, in effect, is the claim that is embodied in the philosophical contrast between 'mental states' and 'behaviour', according to which we do not, strictly speaking, *see* the joy in another's face or the anger in another's eyes: according to which, since 'all that we strictly speaking see of others is the movements of their bodies', all judgements about their thoughts and feelings are the result of an inference – as my judgement that there is an animal in that box is a result of an inference from the funny way the box is moving. We should demand strong arguments before we accept these models.

We will be returning, in Chapter 7, to the Wittgensteinian approach, which gives a central place to the notion of a *human being*. The discussion there will fill in some important gaps in the treatment of the present chapter. Some readers may wish to move straight on to that chapter, returning later to the intervening chapters, in which we will be looking at a very different approach.

Further reading

The connection between mental states and behaviour is given a fundamental place in Gilbert Ryle's enormously influential, and very readable, *The Concept of Mind*; the first chapter of this book gives a good picture of the fundamental defect that Ryle finds in the Cartesian view. A more recent criticism of Descartes' view, in much the same spirit as Ryle's, can be found in Anthony Kenny, *The Metaphysics of Mind*. For a brief, and very helpful, discussion of the connection between mental states and behaviour see Stuart Hampshire, 'Feeling and Expression', in Jonathan Glover (ed.), *The Philosophy of Mind*. I discuss certain aspects of the connection in my paper 'The Mind, the Brain and the Face'.

The connection between mental states and behaviour is also central in Ludwig Wittgenstein's *Philosophical Investigations*. In the discussion of private language in sections 3 and 4 of this chapter I am simply attempting to reproduce what I take to be a line of thought presented by Wittgenstein (roughly in paragraphs 243–317 of the *Philosophical Investigations*). But Wittgenstein's writing is very difficult, and the interpretation, especially of these sections of his work, highly controversial. Accessible treatments of this topic can be found in

Oswald Hanfling, *Wittgenstein's Later Philosophy*, chapter 5, Marie McGinn, *Wittgenstein and the Philosophical Investigations*, chapter 4, and Fergus Kerr, *Theology After Wittgenstein*, chapter 6. For a very brief general introduction to Wittgenstein's thinking on 'human nature' see P.M.S. Hacker, *Wittgenstein*.

For a readable, and illuminating, discussion of our knowledge of others, and the difficulties that may be involved here, see Ilham Dilman, *Love and Human Separateness*. Oliver Sacks' sensitive and fascinating discussion of autism can be found in the title essay of his collection of papers *An Anthropologist on Mars*.

5
The Material Mind

1. The mind–brain identity thesis

In Chapter 4 I presented a criticism of the way in which the Cartesian approach gives absolute priority to the first person point of view. Now I suggested that there is, in contemporary philosophy, another, quite different, line of criticism of the Cartesian view. This approach sees the fundamental defect in Cartesianism as lying, not in the views it implies concerning the *meaning* of our talk about people and their mental states, but rather in its claim about what kinds of thing exist. Descartes' central error, on this view, lies in his suggestion that, in addition to the physical bodies recognized by the sciences, there are also non-material entities with which some of those physical bodies are closely causally linked.

Many now feel that that is a view that we have no reason to accept, and, indeed, very good reason to reject. The reasons for rejecting it are to be found in science. At a very general level we can say first that the sciences are deeply committed to the principle that all changes in the physical world can be explained entirely in terms of other, prior changes in the physical world. Now if the Cartesian view was correct there would be changes at some point in the brain that could *not* be explained in terms of prior physical causes; for their immediate cause would be an event in the non-physical mind.

Of course, the fact – if it is a fact – that the sciences are deeply committed to this principle does not show that the principle is true. But, it might be argued, we have quite powerful grounds for thinking that it *is* true. It has often enough been argued in the past that there are features of the world that could never be explained without postulating the intervention of some external, non-material force. And yet time and again these claims have been shown to be ill-founded. Darwin's theory of evolution provides a relatively recent, and particularly dramatic, example of this. Now no doubt the attempt to provide physical explanations of human behaviour, and of human brain activity, has a long way to go. For all that, has not enough progress been made to suggest that there is, at least, no reason to assume that there is some obstacle, in principle, to the completion of the project in this area too?

Descartes knew enough physiology to know that what emotions and sensations we feel is, in some particularly immediate way, dependent on what happens in the brain. He points out, for example, that if I receive an injury to my hand, but the nerves that run from my hand to my brain are severed, I will feel no pain. But he does not conclude that the pain is a state of the brain, for he suggests that:

> ... the movements which are thus excited in the brain by the nerves, variously affect the soul or mind, which is intimately conjoined with the brain, according to the diversity of the motions themselves. And the diverse affections of the mind or thoughts that immediately arise from these motions, are called perceptions of the senses, or, as we commonly speak, sensations. (Descartes, 1644, p. 215)

These sensations, in turn, produce other motions in the brain, which have effects on the nerves, and so on in a way that ultimately results in a sharp withdrawal of my hand and a cry of pain from my mouth. But what conclusion should we draw if contemporary science suggests that one of the steps in Descartes' story – that which involves the non-material 'soul or mind' – is a myth?

One possible conclusion would be this: science has undermined, or at least may in time undermine, our normal idea that people have minds. 'Folk psychology' – the common-sense framework within which we understand each other, within which we explain and predict the behaviour of ourselves and others – is a pre-scientific theory that could be shown to be, in part or wholly, false by the discovery of explanations of our behaviour in exclusively physical terms. Our everyday idea that the behaviour of people is often the product of beliefs, desires, intentions and so on would be shown to be simply false if all human behaviour could be explained in terms of internal physiology. And science could establish that all human behaviour *can* be explained in such terms, much as it has shown us that the emergence of human beings can be explained without postulating a divine creator, or that the spread of disease can be explained without postulating witchcraft or other forms of supernatural forces.

While suggestions of this kind have been defended with sophisticated arguments, they have seemed to most philosophers to be preposterous. An alternative conclusion, one that in one form or another has seemed hugely attractive, is this: sensations and so on are not states of (affections of) a non-material mind, but, rather, states of the brain. That is not to deny that people have minds; nor is it to deny that people have thoughts, sensations and so on. It is simply to tell us something about what these things are. Just as science has shown us that lightning is an electrical discharge and that water is H_2O, so it has shown us – or at least may well do in time – that sensations are brain processes.

But can this possibly be right? After all, it is clear that people said of themselves 'I am in pain', or of others 'She is in pain', long before they knew anything about what goes on in the brain when someone is in pain. Surely, then, it cannot be correct to suggest that a pain is a brain process; for that would imply, absurdly, that people were saying that certain brain processes were occurring, even though they knew nothing about brain processes!

We see the confusion in this objection when we recognize that the mind–brain identity thesis does not involve a claim about the *meaning* of, for example, the word 'pain'. The words 'He is in pain' do not mean the same as the words 'His C-fibres are firing'. But it does not follow that pain is not a firing of C-fibres. For, all that the latter claim involves is the insistence that the two expressions 'pain' and 'C-fibre firing' refer to the same event. Similarly, the word 'lightning' does not mean the same as the words 'electrical discharge', even though, as a matter of fact, the two expressions refer to the same event. Again, the words 'Tony Blair' and the words 'The Prime Minister of Great Britain' do not mean the same; though as things are just now they do refer to the same individual. It is no objection to the claim that 'Tony Blair is the Prime Minister' that there may be people who can speak about Tony Blair and yet have no idea what a prime minister is, let alone that he is one. It is the same with pain and the firing of C-fibres.

This is connected with the fact that those who defend the mind–brain identity thesis insist that it is not for the philosopher to prove that, for example, pain is the firing of C-fibres. That is a task for the scientist – just as it was a task for the scientist to establish that lightning is an electrical discharge. For all that, we can legitimately ask the philosopher what kind of empirical evidence would provide support for such an identity claim. Now a natural response to that question is, perhaps, this: we would have powerful grounds for the claim that, for example, pain is the firing of C-fibres if it was found that whenever someone is in pain her C-fibres are firing.

Any answer of that form would clearly need a bit of refining. Whenever someone is in pain her heart is beating; yet that, presumably, does nothing to suggest that pain is a beating heart. Perhaps refinements to meet this kind of point can be made. It seems likely, however, that whatever refinements of that form are introduced we will be left with another problem: namely, would not such a correlation be equally consistent with the suggestion that there is a close *causal* connection, rather than an *identity*, between pain and the firing of C-fibres? After all, we cannot conclude from the fact that there is a close correlation between wind and leaves falling off trees that wind just is leaves falling off trees.

There is another problem that has played a crucial role in persuading many philosophers that the mind–brain identity theory as I have presented it has little future. It has been argued that there are powerful reasons for supposing that no such correlations of the kind discussed will be found. There are, it is argued, philosophical grounds for thinking that there is no unique brain event correlated with, for example, the mental event of being in pain; or, to take a rather different kind of example, with the mental event of being suddenly struck by the thought that one's cheque may have bounced. Now if that is so, then it is not simply that we could not have *grounds for accepting* any identity claim of the form: pain is a firing of C-fibres. No identity claim of that form – one that maintains that a certain type of mental event, for example pain, is one and the same thing as a certain type of physical event – could be true. The idea that mental states and events could, in that sense, be *reduced* to physical states and events would be undermined.

We will look in section 5 of the next chapter at one form of the argument mentioned in the previous paragraph. (If you want to pursue this issue now you could look ahead to subsection (i) of Chapter 6 section 5.) For the moment, I want to turn to a different form of materialism: one that may be in a much stronger position at this point.

2. Functionalism (the causal theory of the mind)

I have – in Chapter 4, and in the first section of this chapter – distinguished two general lines of attack on the Cartesian position. Both reach a conclusion that could be formulated in this way: a person is an extended, tangible being that exists in the same world as that of tables, trees and mountains. Yet the kind of criticism each makes of the Cartesian view is very different. It is, in a surprising way, possible that each group will regard its own revision of the traditional view as far more radical than that of the others.

Defenders of the mind–brain identity thesis might say that the Ryle/Wittgenstein criticism of Chapter 4 only concerns the *meanings of words* – in particular, the meaning of our mental vocabulary – while their own criticism calls for a change in our understanding of *what actually exists*. And surely it is revisions in our views about what actually exists that are the really radical ones.

Those who follow in the footsteps of Wittgenstein and Ryle tend to see the matter rather differently. The shift in view about what actually exists is, they may say, a mere detail in comparison with what the identity theorist shares with Descartes. Thus, the identity theory, as it has so far been presented, leaves open the possibility that the first person point of view has the kind of priority it is given in the Cartesian position. It seems to commit itself to the 'Cartesian' claim that the real person is something other than the complete human being that we actually see when we 'meet another person'; and, with this, it commits itself to the view that thought, emotion, sensation and so on are states, not of the *human being*, but of an entity – 'the mind' – that is in some sense lodged in the human being. It differs from Descartes' view simply in its insistence that the relevant entity is a material, rather than a non-material, thing.

By the end of this book you may have your own view as to which of these ways of viewing the matter we should favour. In any case, I want to turn now to a more recent development in the argument. Over the last thirty years there has emerged a form of materialism that can, perhaps, offer us what is best in each of the lines of argument we have considered. This view – known as 'functionalism' – draws on the thought developed in the previous chapter: the thought that there must be a close connection between the *meanings* of words such as 'anger' and 'pain' and the forms of behaviour in which anger and pain are characteristically manifested. But it draws too on a current scientific understanding of what it is reasonable to suppose exists.

Suppose that, impressed by the idea of a connection of meaning between talk about mental states and certain patterns of behaviour, one went on to look (as I suggested that we need not) for some form of 'analysis' of mental talk in terms of behaviour. The simplest kind of connection that we might look for there would be this: to say that 'He has a pain in his foot' is to say that he is crying out, clutching his foot, that he limps when he walks, and so on. Statements about a person's mental states simply *are* statements about that person's behaviour. The pain or anger is not something that lies behind the pained or angry behaviour to which only the individual herself has direct access. The pain or anger simply *is* the behaviour.

That, 'behaviourist', view is obviously very crude. Two, though not perhaps the only two, objections that we might raise against it are these. First, it makes perfectly good sense to suppose that a person should be in pain or angry – or, more obviously still, that a person should believe that Labour will win the next election – without this being manifested in her behaviour. And second, it is a central feature of our normal thought that a person's pains, anger, beliefs and so on can explain her behaviour. That, we might say, is a feature of the meaning of our mental states talk. Thus, our normal ways of speaking about mental states involve the idea that mental states, rather than being identical with behaviour, in some sense lie behind it and cause it. And so the simple behaviourist view cannot be correct as an account of the normal meaning of our talk.

Now functionalism attempts to offer an account of the meaning of our mental vocabulary that corrects these deficiencies in a simple behaviourism. According to functionalism, the meaning of a term such as 'pain' or 'anger' incorporates a reference to the behaviour in which pain or anger is characteristically manifested; but not in a way that involves identifying the mental state with the behaviour. As the view can be expressed: the mental lies behind behaviour, but it is defined in terms of its effects on behaviour. As D.M. Armstrong has expressed it:

> The mental, I hold, has no sort of overlap at all with behaviour. The mental is all within. Nevertheless, the mental has logical links to behaviour. For it is defined in terms of its causal role, and that causal role is spelt out by reference to behaviour (including relations to stimuli). There is a conceptual connection, a subtle form of necessary connection, holding between mental phenomena and behaviour. (Armstrong, 1984, p. 147)

Consider an analogy. When we describe a particular substance, for example arsenic, as a 'poison' we are identifying it in terms of its normal effects. A 'poison' by *definition* characteristically has certain effects. Thus, there is no room for the sceptical question: are those substances, such as arsenic and methylated spirits, that generally make people sick when they swallow them poisonous? For that a particular substance characteristically has these effects is just what we mean in calling it 'poisonous'. For all that, the poisonous substance is not itself the effect: that is, the sickness. The poison is the substance that *causes* the sickness. And this substance has a nature of its own; a nature that it is the business of science to investigate.

Consider another example. Suppose that we come across a new disease. We initially identify it solely in terms of a clear syndrome of symptoms: people develop a severe rash on the face, suffer from violent headaches and some loss of hearing, and so on. Doctors know that some virus is responsible for this syndrome of symptoms, but they know nothing more about the virus. We can imagine that they introduce a term, say 'blick', which means: 'The virus – whatever it may turn out to be – that is responsible for these symptoms.' The virus is, then, defined in terms of its effects. But it is distinct from these effects. It has a nature of its own.

Similarly, David Lewis, another prominent exponent of the functionalist approach, writes:

> Our view is that the concept of pain, or indeed of any other experience or mental state, is the concept of a state that occupies a certain causal role, a state with certain typical causes and effects. It is the concept of a state apt for being caused by certain stimuli and apt for causing certain behaviour. (Lewis, 1994, p. 418)

Thus, a pain is, by definition, an internal state of a person that typically causes people to – or, perhaps, 'inclines this person to' – cry out, clutch or rub part of their body, and so on. Anger is, by definition, an internal state of a person that typically causes people to go red in the face, shout at the smallest provocation, and so on. Mental states are defined in terms of their typical effects. So there is no danger – as there was with dualism – that I might be hopelessly wrong about the mental life of others; that what causes them to cry out and so on is, typically, not pain at all. For, according to functionalism, whatever internal state of the other has a tendency to cause that person to behave in the relevant ways is, by definition, pain. Nevertheless, the pain is distinct from the behaviour. It is an internal state, that has a nature of its own.

Functionalism, as I have so far explained it (what Armstrong calls 'the causal theory of the mind'), is not yet a materialist view. As Lewis says:

> When we describe mental state M as the occupant of the M-role, that is…a topic-neutral description. It says nothing about what sort

of state it is that occupies the role. It might be a non-physical or a physical state, and if it is physical it might be a state of neural activity in the brain, or a pattern of currents and charges on a silicon chip, or the jangling of an enormous assemblage of beer cans. (Lewis, 1994, p. 418)

Lewis adds, however, that '[w]e know enough to rule out the chip and the cans, and to support the hypothesis that what occupies the role is some pattern of neural activity'. For, as Armstrong argues:

... the causal theory of the mind does lead naturally on to a materialist theory of the mind. For suppose that we consider all the outward physical behaviour of human beings, and other higher animals, which we take to be mind-betokening. In the light of our current knowledge, it seems quite likely that the *sole* causes of this behaviour are external physical stimuli together with internal physiological processes, in particular physiological processes in the central nervous system. But if we accept this premiss on grounds of general scientific plausibility, and also accept the causal theory of the mind, the mental must in fact be physiological. (Armstrong, 1984, pp. 157–8)

3. A doubt about the materialist argument

In a recent introduction to the philosophy of mind, on which I have drawn in my presentation of functionalism, it is remarked that:

The issue for us, as for the great majority of contemporary philosophers, is no longer whether physicalism in our very general sense is true but rather what more specific brand or sub-variety of physicalism is defensible. (Smith and Jones, 1986, p. 180)

This may well be true of, at any rate, philosophers in the English-speaking tradition. Just how much truth there is in it will depend on precisely what the force of the term 'physicalism' is. But we will return to that. In this section I want to raise some doubts about what is, perhaps, the most persuasive form of the physicalist (materialist) argument. This argument might be summarized in this way:

It is a crucial feature of our normal thought that a person's anger explains certain patterns in her behaviour. (The functionalist suggests that anger can actually be *defined* in these terms.) But our current knowledge of the achievements of science makes it overwhelmingly likely that all human behaviour can be explained in terms of brain states. This means that we must either say that our normal, everyday, idea is just wrong; that is, that science has shown that it is brain states, not anger, that are the real explanation of the behaviour. Or we must say that anger is a brain state, in this way reconciling our normal thought with the science.

An analogy would be this. Suppose that you are convinced that the head of the department of French was the sole murderer. (He is the explanation of this man's death.) I have good evidence that the local MP was the sole murderer. There is one way in which we can both be right: if the head of the department of French *is* the local MP.

When presenting the argument it is important to keep the following point in mind. The argument does not appeal to claims about what explains our *mental* states: what explains, for example, our anger. Establishing that all mental states are caused by brain states would not be enough to establish materialism; for to say that one thing is *caused by* another is not at all to say that the one thing just *is* the other. Thus even a dualist could allow that all mental states are caused by brain states (adding that the mental state is a quite distinct, non-material, state.) The argument appeals, rather, to the 'common-sense view' that anger is the cause of – that is, the explanation of – the *behaviour*, while science insists that it is brain states that are the cause of the behaviour. It is in order to reconcile these two claims that we must conclude that the anger is a brain state.

I am, for the moment, going to assume that the first half of the functionalist account – the claim, outlined in the previous section, about the *meaning* of our mental terms – is basically correct. My question will be: does this claim, combined with our current knowledge of the achievements of science, make it likely that mental states are states of the brain? Now a proper discussion of that question would require a knowledge of the achievements of science that I do not possess. But there is, I want to suggest, an illusion here that can make this defence of materialism seem far more plausible than it should. The illusion depends on an ambiguity in the term 'behaviour': an ambiguity that also played a crucial role in our consideration of the argument from analogy.

It is suggested that our current knowledge of the achievements of science makes it overwhelmingly likely that all human behaviour can be explained in terms of brain states. Now what exactly does the term 'behaviour' mean here? If it means 'movements of the human body' the claim is plausible. Scientists are, of course, nowhere near producing such explanations. But they have taken some steps down this path, and the success of science in other areas in explaining the way bodies move makes it plausible to suggest that in principle it can do the same here. Thus, if we want to explain why his hand moved up we might do this in terms of the fact that this muscle contracted, that was caused by this brain mechanism, and so on. Similarly, with the rising of the corner of this fleshy strip near the top of his body (his mouth). It is, then, perhaps plausible to suggest that it will be possible to explain in physical terms – in terms of what takes place in the brain – all human behaviour described in terms of movements of matter. The traditional dualist is committed to the denial of this. But modern science makes that implausible.

Consider now our normal explanations of behaviour. What is it that we generally think is to be explained in terms of a person's anger or beliefs? We can say 'his behaviour'. But what the term means here is, on the face of it, quite different. Our normal descriptions of behaviour are in terms of *action* and *expression*. In the final section of Chapter 4 I gave the following examples: 'He opened the window and smiled at the woman outside', 'He checkmated her in five moves', 'He danced a highland fling', 'He glared at her with a scowl on his face', 'She said that it was time to go', 'He got divorced', 'Her face lit up with joy'. Now it is behaviour described in terms of action and expression that we normally think is to be explained in terms of anger, pain and so on. We ask 'Why was he so rude to her?', and receive the reply 'He was angry'. We ask 'Why did he vote for the Conservatives?', and receive the reply 'He believed they would handle the economy better'. What we are struck by, and so want explained, is not the particular movements that his body made. Those movements in another context would not have been rudeness; and many quite different movements in this context could be rudeness. It is under the description 'He was rude to her' that we think his behaviour is to be explained in terms of his anger: under what we might call a description in 'human terms'.

With this in mind we can return to the functional definition of 'anger': anger is that state of a person that characteristically brings about behaviour of such-and-such kinds. To be at all plausible as a definition of what we mean by the term 'anger' we need to take the term 'behaviour' in what I have called the 'human' sense. For example, 'anger' is that state of a person that typically causes a person to do things of the following kinds: scowl at anyone who gets in his way, be much ruder than he usually is, fumble simple tasks that he normally performs without difficulty, and so on. Not: 'anger' is that state of a person that typically causes his left arm to rise rapidly through a 90° arc, the corners of his lips to stretch between 3 and 5 mm. wider than usual, and so on. As I have stressed before, there is a clear sense in which we do not even notice many of the ways in which another's body moves in *that* sense; and these movements are not, in any case, what generally interests us in the 'behaviour' of others. It is, then, extremely implausible to suggest that the meaning of the term 'anger' is linked, in the way that is central to functionalism, with 'behaviour' understood in *those* terms.

Now if this is correct then it appears that what we generally, at an everyday level, think is explained by – caused by – 'mental states' is *not the same thing* as that which we have good reason to suppose science will be able to explain in physiological terms. So we can agree that 'anger is the state that brings about such and such behaviour' without agreeing that the current scientific knowledge makes it plausible to think that anger will turn out to be a brain state. For we have no reason to think that science will be able to explain *action and expression* in neurophysiological terms. (At least we do not have the very obvious kind of reason that I have discussed.)

Consider an analogy. I point at a man walking down the road and ask 'What is the explanation of that?' The pointing gesture does not show what I want explained. He is walking in a cheerful way down the left-hand side of Bridge St at 10.00 at night. The explanation of his walking in a cheerful way ('He has just won the pools') may be quite unconnected with the explanation of his walking on the left-hand side ('It is safer'). We have a single event here: a man walking in a cheerful way down the left-hand side of Bridge Street at 10.00 at night. But what counts as an explanation depends on what it was about the event that struck us. It was a certain aspect of what happened – that is to say, what happened under a certain description – that puzzled us and so we want explained. And there need be no link between the explanations under the different descriptions. Thus, it would clearly not do to argue:

> The explanation of his walking in a *cheerful* way down the left-hand side of Bridge Street is that he has just won the pools.
> The explanation of his walking in a cheerful way down the *left-hand side* of Bridge Street is that it is safer.

So, the fact that he has just won the pools must be the *same* fact as the fact that the left-hand side is safer.

Similarly, it is not under the description in terms of movements of bodies in space that we are generally struck by another's behaviour, and so want it explained. So an explanation under that description may be quite unconnected with our normal explanations. No explanation of why a person's body is moving in a certain way will be an explanation of why he is acting as he is. For the same bodily movements are compatible with an indefinite range of actions. A man whose finger is moving slowly down may be squashing a slug or launching a missile. In explaining why his finger is moving like that we are not explaining why he is doing what he is. So we cannot argue:

> The explanation of his finger moving slowly down is that neuron x fired in his brain.
> The explanation of his launching a missile is that he wanted to show Colonel Gadaffi that he can't play games with the United States.
> So, the firing of neuron x and his want must be the *same* event.

4. A materialist response

It must be said that the materialists whom I am discussing tend not to be very impressed by this kind of argument. I am not quite sure just *why* they do not find it compelling. Perhaps one reason is this: they cannot see how any consideration of this kind could show materialism to be false. But to this it must be replied that the argument is not intended to show that materialism is false. It is simply intended to show that one form of *argument for materialism* – one that I suspect has a powerful hold on the thought of many of us – is not valid.

There is a response that goes deeper than this which needs to be discussed in some detail. The response has two strands that I will present separately, and then show how, in combination, they might provide the materialist with a response to the objections of the previous section.

In my discussion of the argument for materialism I moved fairly freely between speaking of the 'explanation' of what someone did and the 'cause' of what he did. But it is possible that in doing so I was side-stepping a difficulty. Consider an explosion that took place at 9.00 a.m. outside Lampeter Co-op. As in previous examples, while we have a single event here, the explanation of the explosion's taking place *at 9.00 a.m.* may be quite different from its taking place *outside the Co-op*. It took place outside the Co-op because the gas mains had been weakened by years of heavy traffic passing above it; it took place at 9.00 a.m. because that is when someone dropped a lighted match. But suppose we ask of this single event – the explosion that took place at 9.00 a.m. outside Lampeter Co-op – what its *causes* were. In that case we will have to speak both of the passing traffic weakening the pipes and of the dropped match; and, depending on how much detail we wish to provide and how far back we want to trace the causal chain, perhaps a good bit more besides.

We might put the matter this way: an explanation is something that removes a puzzle. Now different people can be puzzled in different ways about a single event: one is puzzled by *when* the explosion happened, the other by *where* it happened. Where that is so, what counts as an explanation for one – what removes his puzzle – may not count as an explanation for another. Thus, in giving an explanation of an event we pick out those of its causes that were relevant to the particular features of the event that puzzled us. By contrast, the *causes* of an event are not, in this way, relative to what we found interesting or puzzling about what happened; and so in giving the cause of an event it is quite irrelevant how the event in question is picked out through our description.

We will see the significance of this after we have considered a second strand in the materialist's response to my suggestions in the previous section. It may be argued that, while it is true that there are two different kinds of description that can be given of 'behaviour', these two forms of description are descriptions of a single thing. There is a single event that can be described either as 'Jones voting for the Conservatives' or as 'Jones' hand moving through space in such-and-such ways'; again, there is a single event that can be described either as 'Mary smiled at John' or as 'The corners of Mary's lips stretched and rose by 15 mm while Mary's eyes … '. As we might put this: all actions are physical movements.

The materialist argument can now unfold in this way. It is a crucial feature of our normal thought that when we explain what a person did in terms of her emotions, beliefs, desires and so on, we are speaking of factors that are *causes* of her behaviour. But it is plausible to suppose that all the causes of the physical movements of a human body are purely physical. Now since 'the things that people do' are one and the same thing as 'the physical movements that their bodies make' the above two assumptions can only be reconciled if every mental state is one and the same thing as some physical state.

What should we make of this argument? My own answer is: we should be a little wary of it. For the argument turns on three ideas that, while I am reluctant to say are clearly false, I am equally reluctant to say are clearly true. These are the ideas that:

(i) It is a crucial feature of our normal thought that when we explain what a person did in terms of her emotions, beliefs, desires and so on, we are speaking of factors that are causes of her behaviour.

(ii) It makes sense to speak of 'all the causes' of some event.

(iii) All actions are physical movements.

We must consider these in turn.

(i) *Is* it a crucial feature of our normal thought that when we speak of the emotions, desires or beliefs that explain why someone did what she did we are speaking of *causes* of her behaviour? Well, my sense is that in practice we do not tend to express matters in that way. If I am asked 'Why did you smile?' I might reply 'I thought what you said was funny'; if asked 'Why did you vote Conservative?' I might reply 'I thought we should give them just five more years to see if they could get it right'. But if I was asked 'What caused you to smile?' or 'What caused you to vote Conservative?' I might be puzzled. The suggestion that something *caused* me to smile or to vote Conservative seems to carry the implication that I didn't have any good reason for doing so: that it was some non-rational mechanism – some force that took hold of me – that explains my behaviour.

Perhaps, then, it can be argued that *causes* are only one among a variety of kinds of factor that can feature in the explanation of an event. While my beliefs and desires play a crucial role in the explanation of my behaviour, the role that they standardly play is not that of being causes. Beliefs, desires and so on, are, in normal cases, *reasons*, not causes, for what I do. If that is correct, then the materialist argument is defused. Even if all of the *causes* of my behaviour are purely physical there is room for mental states in the explanation of my behaviour without those being physical states.

Now philosophers have argued that, despite the connotations of the use of the word 'cause' in normal speech, it *is* a central feature of our normal thought that when we explain someone's behaviour by citing emotions, desires or beliefs we are speaking of 'causes' of their behaviour. I cannot argue here that they are *wrong* about that. I don't know how to! But I don't know how to in part because I am really not clear what is at issue here. If the philosophers who made this kind of claim were suggesting that all of our behaviour was the product of non-rational mechanisms – the product of forces that take hold of us – then I would be fairly clear what they were saying; and I think I would have some idea how to reply to it. (We will consider issues in this area in Chapter 9.) But that is not what is at issue here. It is assumed that our normal distinction between cases in which a person did something because he saw good reason to do it and cases in which something *made* him do it is quite in order; but it is added that even in the former cases beliefs, desires and so on are *causes* of the behaviour.

Philosophers who have defended this claim have offered accounts of what it amounts to and why we should accept it, and I certainly cannot do justice to their arguments here. Rather than press this point further, I want to raise another consideration that may create difficulties for the materialist argument at this point.

(ii) The materialist argument aims to show that if some mental state, say a belief or desire, is to be among the causes of some movement of my body it can only be so by *being* some physical state or event. To establish this conclusion appeal is made to the claim that: all the causes of the physical movements of a human body are purely physical. If *all* the causes of the movements of a human body are purely physical then a mental state can only be one of the causes if it itself is one of those purely physical states.

But do we really have a firm grasp on the notion of '*all* the causes' of some event? Consider an example from a different area. Suppose that we ask: is the fact that a gigantic meteor did not land on Edinburgh in 1948 among the causes of my existence? (I was born in Edinburgh some time after that.) Well, if a gigantic meteor *had* landed on Edinburgh in 1948 I would never have been born. That this did not happen is a necessary condition of my being born. Is it one of the 'causes' of my being born? Well, this much is, I think, true: we can imagine circumstances in which the fact that a meteor didn't land on a city would quite naturally be offered as part of the explanation of someone's being born. (Consider the way in which we can offer the fact that it *didn't* rain for two months as part of the explanation of the failure of the crops.) For all that, we would never, in normal circumstances, dream of mentioning it in a list of causes of my birth.

Are we, then, to say that the meteor's not landing on Edinburgh is one of the causes of my birth? I have very little idea how to answer that question – and I regard this failure as a mark of philosophical good sense. (Others will disagree!) In any case, if we say that it *is* one of the causes of my birth, then we are going to have to accept that there is no such thing as a list of 'all of the causes' of some event – for there is no limit on the number of factors that *could* be mentioned, in the same kind of way as the absence of the meteor could be mentioned. If we say that it is *not* one of the causes of my birth, then we are, I think, going to have to accept that there is no sharp way of drawing a distinction between what are and are not causes of some event: that is, no sharp way of doing so outside the context of a particular interest in the event. Either way, the idea of 'all of the causes' of an event, which plays a crucial role in this argument for materialism, may lack the clarity that is called for in the argument.

(iii) The third idea that I suggested we need to consider here was the claim that: all actions are physical movements. This claim was needed in order to make the move from the hypothesis that 'All bodily movements have purely physical causes' to the conclusion that 'All actions have purely physical causes'. What should we make of the claim? Consider an example. Jones shoots and fatally wounds Smith, who dies three days later. Is Jones' act of killing Smith one and the same occurrence as the physical movement that his finger made in pulling the trigger – as the car crash I saw last Tuesday is one and the same event as the accident in which the History teacher injured his leg? On the face of it there is a difficulty here. The car crash that I saw last Tuesday can only be the same event as the accident in which the History teacher injured his leg if the one occurred at the same time and place as the other. If it turns out that the crash that I saw took place at 11.15 in Harford Square while the one in which the History teacher was injured took place at 2.35, or in some quite different part of town, then we have no choice but to conclude that we have two different accidents here.

So does Jones' killing of Smith occur at the same time and place as the movement of his finger on the trigger? Well, where and when *does* Jones' killing of Smith occur? Suppose that Jones shot Smith on Monday, but Smith did not die until Thursday. Did Jones kill Smith on Monday? One might, very reasonably, think that that can't be right since that would imply that Smith lived for three days after he had been killed! It is true that, at least in the movies, the fatally wounded gangster says to his assailant 'You've killed me'; but one might think it obvious that, in one way, these words cannot be taken at face value. Similar questions arise when we ask '*Where* did Jones kill Smith?'

Now there has been considerable philosophical dispute about how these questions are to be answered; and reasons have been offered for thinking that we *must* answer them in a certain way – for example, by saying that Jones killed Smith on Monday – if we are to avoid other difficult questions. We cannot explore these issues further here. We need only note that we will only be able to agree that Jones' act of killing Smith is one and the same event as the physical movement of Jones' finger on the trigger if the first occurred at the same time (and place) as the second: that is, at a certain particular instant on Monday. And it is far from clear that our normal ways of speaking of what people do allows for this to be said.

Are all actions physical movements? I do not suggest that the above considerations show decisively that they are not. Indeed, my own inclination is not so much to *deny* that they are as to suspect that there is something odd in the insistence that there must be a 'Yes or no' answer here. Compare: is a wooden ship that has had all of its planks changed one by one over a period of twenty years one and the same ship as that with which we started? The correct answer to that question is, I take it, 'Well…' – said in a tone (difficult to capture in print) that makes it clear that anyone who insists on a 'Yes or no' answer to this question is asking for something that he should not want. Our language simply does not dictate one answer rather than another; and, while for certain philosophical purposes it may prove useful to tidy up the language in one way or another, we should not think of this 'tidying up' as a revealing to us of some deep truth about how things are in the world.

I should warn the beginner that those remarks reveal a huge amount about my own philosophical temperament! Philosophers have designed tests by means of which to decide whether or not we should say that two descriptions are descriptions of a single event; and have suggested that if, at certain points, these tests commit us to some counterintuitive claims then that only shows the fallibility of our normal intuitions. As we might put this: while *they* are inclined to judge particular claims in the light of the tests, *I* might be more inclined to judge the tests in the light of the particular claims that issue from them. But large, general questions about the nature of philosophy open up at this point. I can here do no more than alert you to these questions, declare my own viewpoint, and press on.

If there is no straightforward answer to the questions 'Are a person's emotions, beliefs, desires and so on, *causes* of her behaviour?' and 'Are all actions physical movements?' then the route to the claim that mental states are brain states is not straightforward either. I have suggested that the sense in which it is not straightforward is something like this: we should have doubts about whether key words in the discussion are being used in quite their normal way. Now if there are steps in the argument that we can only go along with by allowing a few liberties to be taken with our normal understanding of the ideas of 'cause' and 'sameness' then we should, perhaps, treat the conclusion that, for example, 'His belief that it is Tuesday is a brain state' with caution. To change the example to one that (I am glad to say) we are more likely to find in a piece of popular science writing than in the work of recent philosophers: if someone tells us that 'happiness is a little neurotransmitter called serotonin' we may be excited or alarmed; but if it turns out that too many liberties have been taken on the way to this conclusion we may have to say that the sense, if any, in which the conclusion must be accepted is not quite what it seems.

It has to be said that I have not shown, or even tried to, that philosophers *cannot* give clear, and uncontroversial, meaning to the claims that are crucial to their argument for materialism. I have, at best, done no more than suggest that there may be a bit of work to do here. But making that suggestion is not going to be enough to undermine the persistent pull of materialist styles of thinking. We will have to approach the issues from a slightly different angle in the next chapter.

Further reading

'Eliminative materialism' – the suggestion that 'folk psychology' is a pre-scientific theory that could be shown to be, in part or wholly, false – is defended by P.M. Churchland in 'Eliminative Materialism and the Propositional Attitudes'. Churchland also defends this view, while giving a useful introductory survey of the alternatives, in his *Matter and Consciousness*.

For early presentations of the mind–brain identity thesis see U.T. Place, 'Is Consciousness a Brain Process?', and J.J.C. Smart, 'Sensations and Brain Processes'. For criticisms of this view, of a kind strongly influenced by Wittgenstein, see Norman Malcolm, 'Scientific Materialism and the Identity Theory', and also Norman Malcolm, *Problems of Mind* Part II. In an influential, but difficult, paper Donald Davidson presents an argument against the idea that there are likely to be close correlations between mental events of a particular kind and physical events of a particular kind; and defends a version of the identity thesis that does not require such correlations. See 'Mental Events', in his collection *Essays on Actions and Events*.

A very accessible introductory text in which, after detailed discussions of other views, functionalism is defended is Peter Smith and O.R. Jones, *The Philosophy of Mind: an Introduction*. My presentation of the functionalist view is based primarily on this, and on D.M. Armstrong's contribution to D.M. Armstrong and Norman Malcolm, *Consciousness and Causality*.

In one of my criticisms of the argument for materialism I questioned whether our normal explanations of human actions speak of causes of the action. The most famous defence of the view that they do is in Donald Davidson, 'Actions, Reasons and Causes' in his *Essays on Actions and Events*. In another of my criticisms, the question of the time and place at which a particular action can be said to have occurred emerged as crucial in that it was crucial to the question of whether we could say that actions are physical movements of the body. Again, see Davidson, 'Agency' in his *Essays on Actions and Events*.

A Companion to the Philosophy of Mind, edited by Samuel Guttenplan, contains a number of useful entries on the themes of this and the following chapters. Most relevant for this chapter are those on 'functionalism (1)', 'identity theories' and 'Putnam, Hilary'. Two useful collections of papers that focus, though not exclusively, on themes addressed in this, and the next, chapters are David M. Rosenthal (ed.), *The Nature of Mind* and William C. Lycan (ed.), *Mind and Cognition: a Reader*. The section on 'Functionalist Approaches' in the first of these contains influential papers on functionalism by Hilary Putnam, David Lewis and Ned Block.

C. McDonald, *Mind-Body Identity Theories* is an accessible text that addresses the themes of this chapter.

For criticisms of some of the assumptions that underlie the approach we have been considering see K.V. Wilkes, 'Pragmatics in Science and Theory in Common Sense', R.A. Sharpe, 'The Very Idea of a Folk Psychology', and John Haldane, 'Understanding Folk'.

6
Mental Causation, Supervenience and Physicalism

1. Psychological explanation and the micro-world

Consider the question: do mental states make any difference to anything that happens in the world? On the face of it, it is clear that our normal thought takes it for granted that they do. For example, that oak tree would still be standing had it not been for the fact that Jones wanted to improve the view from his study and so chopped it down. The suggestion that the tree would have come down anyway, whether or not Jones had wanted it to, seems to be, first, false, and, second, in radical conflict with our normal understanding of the position that we occupy in the world.

Yet the idea that our mental states *do* make a difference to what happens in the world might seem to be in severe tension with an assumption that is central to the current 'scientific world-view'. We might formulate the assumption in this way: everything that happens in the physical world has entirely physical causes. But perhaps a more precise and helpful formulation would be this:

> [U]ltimately the world – at least, the physical world – is the way it is because the microworld is the way it is – because there are so many of just these sorts of microentitites (elementary particles, atoms, or what not), and they behave in accordance with just these laws. (Kim, 1991, p. 261)

For example, heating water to 100°C causes it to boil. We take it for granted that there is an explanation of this fact in terms of the particles of which water is composed. The rise in temperature of the water involves an increase in the velocities of the water molecules, which, at a certain point, is sufficient to lead to the ejection of molecules into the air: that is to say, the boiling of the water.

Well, the way I have put that particular example may be scientifically a little naïve. My point is simply that we are assured by science that some story in terms of the particles of which water is composed is available here; and further, the assumption that the behaviour of wholes – such as trees, cars or bodies of water – is ultimately to be explained in terms of their parts is one that, for some reason, seems to come quite naturally to all of us. We take it for granted that the behaviour of the car is entirely dependent on the behaviour of the pistons, gear wheels, and so on; that the behaviour of an individual piston is entirely dependent on the behaviour of the parts of which it is composed; and so on down to some fundamental level which it is the business of our most basic science – presumably physics – to investigate.

Now consider people. A door closes on my hand, and I wince with pain. The wince involves my hand flying back, my eyes closing and certain other distinctive movements in my face, a cry coming from my mouth, and so on. It is central to our normal understanding of such cases that I would not have winced had I not been in pain. Yet the above principle insists that the causes of my body moving in these ways are to be found entirely in the micro-entitites (elementary particles, atoms, or what not) of which my body is composed.

Again, a tree falls. We normally assume that this may be true:

> That oak tree would still be standing had it not been for the fact that Jones wanted to remove it. Jones' desire that it should come down played an essential role in its coming down.

Yet the above principle insists that the causes of the tree coming down are to be found entirely in the realm of the micro-entitites of which physics speaks. The atoms that make up Jones' nerves, muscles, brain and so on will feature in the complete causal account of the tree's falling; but there seems to be no place here for the idea that Jones' desire had an essential role to play.

The worry that arises here can be presented in a slightly different way. One of the concerns of recent work in the philosophy of mind can be formulated like this: what is the relationship between the explanatory stories we tell in our everyday talk about human behaviour and the explanatory stories of the physicist? In the previous chapter I suggested that a certain, simple, view of the relation between these stories could be rejected on the grounds that the explanations offered within the two systems are explanations of different things: roughly, one offers explanations of the actions of human beings, and the other explanations of the movements of human bodies. But to leave the matter there would be to ignore the fact that there is some kind of fairly close relationship between the way in which a person's body moves and what that person is doing. Certainly there is a wide range of ways in which a person's body may move when he is kicking a penalty in football. But the range is not completely unlimited. Thus, suppose that, prior to the time the kick is due, the arrangement of elementary particles in his body and immediate surroundings is such that it is causally inevitable that, at the relevant time, his body will be orientated in the position characteristic of a handstand. In that case it is clear that, however surprising this may be when viewed from the level of our normal understanding of human behaviour, he will not be kicking a penalty at the time in question.

Now we should be struck by the fact that, while life is full of surprises, our normal methods of predicting what people will do are reasonably reliable. I know that she desperately wants that car. When she wins her fortune on the lottery, I predict that she will go out and buy it. And sure enough she does! Why should we be struck by this? Well, it is a widely held assumption that there is another level of prediction and explanation: the level at which the physicist works. Now on the face of it, the world *could* have been such that predictions made at these two levels were rarely in harmony with each other. While, given her wants and her wealth her buying that car seems all but inevitable, given the arrangement of sub-atomic particles in her body and its vicinity it is out of the question: it is inevitable that her body will move in ways that are straightforwardly incompatible with her buying the car. Yet life is not like that. So we must seek an understanding of the relationship between the two systems of prediction and explanation such that we can say that it is not a perpetual fluke that they march in step with each other.

2. Descartes on interaction and the laws of physics

It will be helpful here to consider how Descartes viewed this issue. On Descartes' view, what happens when I swing my arm – say, in chopping down a tree – is this. A mental event of willing takes place in the non-material mind; this brings about a physical event in the pineal gland; and this is the first physical stage in a causal chain that leads to the contraction of certain muscles and so the swinging of my arm. When we say 'He swung his arms in that way because he wanted to chop down the tree' we are saying that the sequence that led to his arms swinging was initiated by a desire to chop down the tree: the desire being a non-material state. Now it seems that if things really did happen in this way then there would be certain physical events in the pineal gland that would be quite inexplicable in physical terms; for what is crucial to their explanation is a *mental* event – and that lies beyond the realm of which the physicist speaks.

While Descartes had a high respect for, and a good knowledge of, the physics of his time, he was not, apparently, troubled by this implication of his view: he was prepared to accept that there are physical events whose causes are not entirely physical. It is, however, important to distinguish this point from another. Descartes insisted that it does not follow from his view that whenever a person acts there is a *violation* of the physical laws of nature: nothing happens that is in any sense excluded by the laws of physics. A rough analogy for the distinction being drawn here can be found in connection with laws of a quite different kind. The law of the land *requires* certain actions, such as wearing a seat belt when driving; and it *forbids* certain other actions, such as theft. But many (indeed, the great bulk) of the things that we do are neither required by, nor forbidden by, the law. Similarly, we might say, with the laws of physics. In a particular set of circumstances, the laws of physics dictate that certain things *must* happen, and that certain other things *cannot* happen. But in addition to these two groups there may be things that *could* happen, even though, if they did, they could not be explained in terms of the laws of physics.

Descartes believed that one physical law that *excludes* certain happenings was what can be called 'the law of conservation of motion'. This holds, roughly, that if one physical body gains or loses speed there must be a 'corresponding' loss or gain in speed in another body. Now one might think that Descartes' account of mind–body interaction is in conflict with this, since one might picture the mind's influence on the body in terms of a mental event 'pushing' a physical particle into motion; and so we would have an increase in motion of a physical particle without any corresponding loss in motion in another physical particle. But, Descartes argues, it does not have to be like that. The action of mind on body might not involve 'pushing a particle into motion', but rather 'diverting the course of a particle that is already in motion'. If it was like that, the non-physical could have effects on the physical without any *violation* of the law of conservation of motion; even though the motion of a particular particle could not be fully *explained* in terms of physical laws.

Unfortunately, Descartes' physics was wrong. What is conserved, according to the physicists, is not simply 'quantity of motion' but 'quantity of motion *in a given direction*'. (That, at least, is how things stood in physics until Einstein; and the change introduced by his thinking does not affect the present line of argument.) Thus, if a billiard ball is at one moment travelling at a certain speed in a northerly direction, and later is travelling at the same speed in a southerly direction, then, according to this principle, there must be some other body that undergoes a 'corresponding' and opposite change in its motion: for example, another billiard ball that was travelling *south* until it collided with this one and bounced back in a northerly direction. Now Descartes' picture of what is involved in mind–body interaction *does* conflict with this principle of conservation; for it involves a particle changing direction without any 'compensating' change in another physical particle.

3. Mind–body supervenience: epiphenomenalism

A different response to this issue involves an appeal to a notion that has played an important role in recent philosophy of mind: that of 'supervenience'. Jaegwon Kim, a philosopher whose name is particularly associated with this approach, formulates the doctrine of mind–body supervenience in this way: 'any two things, or events, that are exactly alike in all physical respects cannot differ in mental respects' (Kim, 1996, p. 148); or, as he also expresses it, 'the mental character of a thing is wholly determined by its physical nature' (Kim, 1994, p. 575).

Consider the following 'small' modification to Descartes' dualism. While 'the mind' is a distinct, non-material realm in which mental events take place, and while changes in the body cause changes in the mind, nothing that happens in the mind has any effects in the physical realm. When my hand gets jammed in a door, this sets up a physical causal chain in my body, which, when it reaches a certain point in my brain, brings about a sensation of pain in the non-material mind. The pain does not, however, in its turn have any effect on the body. The bodily response of wincing has entirely physical causes. For the brain event that causes the pain also has physical effects that ultimately lead to the wince. The mental event – the pain – is, then, an 'epiphenomenon': a shadow cast by what happens in the brain. That is not to deny that it is a real event. It is simply to note that – like a shadow, or an image in a mirror – it does not itself have the power to affect what happens in the physical world.

Similarly, it is an illusion to suppose that my desire to chop down the tree plays any role in bringing about certain movements of my body, or the felling of the tree. The causes of these events are to be found wholly in the non-mental realm: the realm of neuron firings, and so on. The illusion is explained by the fact that the relevant mental event – the desire that the tree be chopped down – and the corresponding physical event – the swinging of my arms that is involved in the felling of the tree – are effects of a common cause – certain neural activity in my brain. So there is a rough correlation between people having a desire to fell a tree and the fellings of trees; just as there is, perhaps, a rough correlation between images in mirrors of vases falling and subsequent smashings of actual vases. In both cases the correlation might tempt us to think that events of the first kind cause events of the second kind. But in the first case, as in the second, we would be wrong.

'Epiphenomenalism' of the above kind involves the idea that the mental is supervenient on the physical: an individual's mental states are wholly determined by the physical states of his body. Thus, if we had two atom-for-atom identical human bodies there would be, associated with those bodies, two minds with identical mental states. While that may not, as it stands, sound too alarming, this view has the consequence that our normal understanding of ourselves and our situation in the world involves a fundamental error: the error of supposing that anything that we think, feel or desire ever makes any difference to anything that happens in the material world. Now you may well feel that this conclusion is a high price to pay for what is, after all, only an assumption: the assumption that all physical events have exclusively physical causes. You would not be alone! But the recent interest in the idea of supervenience has stemmed from the idea that there might be a way of having the assumption without the price.

4. Mind–body supervenience: physicalism

I introduced epiphenomenalism as being one form of the doctrine of supervenience. However, the form of that doctrine that is receiving serious discussion today is, as you might have guessed, very different in character. Two examples from other areas illustrate the possibility of quite different forms of supervenience. Consider first the relation between a painting of a human face and the arrangement of patches of colour of which the painting 'consists'. There is a sense in which, when we look at the painting, we may not notice (at any rate all of) the individual patches of colour. Thus, I might later, when the canvas has been removed, be able to describe in fine detail the expression on the face, and yet be able to tell you little of the form 'There is a circular splash of red two thirds of the way down the canvas…'. For all that, the expression on the face is wholly determined by the arrangement of the colour patches: if we held in our hands another canvas on which there was just the same arrangement of colour patches we would, of necessity, be holding in our hands a painting of a human face bearing just the same expression. The face depicted is, then, supervenient on the arrangement of colour patches on the canvas. However, the *sense* in which the arrangement of colour patches determines the character of the face is very different from that involved in the epiphenomenal view considered above. In the epiphenomenal account mental events were understood to be events that are quite distinct from the physical states by which they are 'determined'; and, with that, the determination was *causal*. The situation is quite different in the case of the painting. There is, it seems, a clear sense in which the painting of the face is nothing over and above the arrangement of colour patches; and, with that, the sense in which the character of the face is 'determined by' the arrangement of patches of colour is 'tighter' than that involved in the causal case. The sense in which there 'could not' be a painting with the same arrangement of colour patches but a different face is not dependent upon the particular laws of nature that operate in the world.

For a second example of an alternative form of supervenience consider the relation between the atoms of which a body of water is composed and the body of water itself. The condition and behaviour of the body of water is wholly determined by the behaviour of the atoms. As with the painting, it cannot be said that the body of water is quite distinct from the 'underlying' arrangement of atoms. With this, the sense in which the behaviour of the water is 'determined by' the behaviour of the atoms is, again, 'tighter' than that involved in the causal account of the mind–body relation. One might wonder if it is quite as tight as the relation between the patches of colour and the painting of a face. But we can leave such details to one side for our present purposes.

Suppose now it was suggested that mental states are supervenient on brain states in *something like* the way in which the face and its expression are supervenient on the arrangement of patches of colour, or the behaviour of the body of water is supervenient on the behaviour of the atoms of which it is composed. Let us not, for the moment, look too hard at just how the analogy might be spelled out. *If* the analogy could be spelled out then we could say that, for example, a particular thought or sensation is 'nothing over and above' its neurophysiological basis in something like the sense in which the painting of the face is nothing over and above the arrangement of colour patches. As the idea is sometimes expressed, the mental is 'composed out of' or 'realized by' the physical – as the painting of the face is composed out of patches of colour or the water is composed out of the atoms.

Now if the connection between a mental state and its physical basis is of *this* kind then, it might be argued, we are not confronted with a problem about how mental states can have effects in the material world: how, for example, Jones' desire to chop down that tree can lead to the chopping down of the tree. Compare a case in which a bowl of ice cream placed in a hot room melts. We can allow that it is the action of the air molecules on the ice cream molecules that is doing the fundamental causal work without implying that there is any confusion in our normal idea that it was the heat in the room that caused the ice cream to melt; for the heat in the room is nothing over and above the high velocity of air molecules in the room, and the melting of the ice cream nothing over and above the loosening of the bonds between the molecules of which it is composed. Similarly, Jones' desire to chop down the tree is nothing over and above the physical condition of his brain that is its basis. Thus, to say that it is the latter that is doing the fundamental causal work is not to deny that the desire played a causal role in the chopping down of the tree.

5. Two doubts about supervenience physicalism

We need not explore the question of how, if at all, this version of physicalism differs from that discussed in the previous chapter. I will not, either, pursue a range of important questions about the precise form of the supervenience envisaged in this approach. I offered as analogies the relation between a portrait and the patches of paint of which it is composed, and that between a body of water and the molecules of which it is composed. It may have struck you, however, that there are significant differences between those examples; and, further, that it is not clear precisely how *either* of them provides a model in terms of which we might understand the relation between a mental state and its 'physical basis'. Rather than pursue these issues, I want briefly to raise two doubts about this whole approach.

(i) The first doubt is a widely discussed objection to the central claim of mind–body supervenience. To say that mental states are supervenient on physical states is to say that 'any two things, or events, that are exactly alike in all physical respects cannot differ in mental respects', or that 'the mental character of a thing is wholly determined by its physical nature'. Consider a woman who is suddenly struck by the thought that her cheque may have bounced. According to the supervenience thesis as we have been understanding it, any exact physical replica of this woman would necessarily also be having this thought. Now consider a nineteenth-century woman living a Stone Age life in some remote valley that has had no contact with the wider world. However unlikely it may be, there is, presumably, no physical law that rules out the possibility that her body should be an exact physical replica of that of the woman who has the thought about her cheque. But would it be the case – *could* it be the case – that this woman too was being struck by the thought that her cheque may have bounced? On the face of it, it is not clear what *sense* it would make to suggest that this woman might be having that thought. Whatever thought she is having, we cannot characterize it in *that* way.

The force of this point might be brought out by the following comparison. We have had occasion to note that our actions are only the actions that they are within the context of certain surroundings. However a person's body may be moving he is only checkmating his opponent in a game of chess if the game of chess has been invented, he has been playing a game of chess, the pieces are now arranged in a certain way on the board, and so on. Now an analogous point has application in connection with our ascriptions of thoughts. Confronted with an old man, suffering from senile dementia, who has not had a cheque book for years, it is only in a 'play acting' way that we say of him that 'He is worried that his cheque may have bounced'. This is not to say that his concern is not to be taken seriously; it is to say something about the *kind* of seriousness that is appropriate. Now the situation of the Stone Age woman is a good bit more extreme than this. She may frown, shake her head, and mutter the words 'Oh dear. Is there enough money in my account?' But given the context of her life – the lack of an institution of banking in her society, the fact that she doesn't know what a cheque book is (not to mention the question of whether she speaks English) – that is hardly sufficient to give sense to the suggestion that she was suddenly struck by the thought that her cheque may have bounced.

If that line of argument is correct a person's thoughts are not supervenient on the physical states of her body. It is not true that 'any two things, or events, that are exactly alike in all physical respects cannot differ in mental respects'. For the idea that a person is having a certain thought – for example, that her cheque may have bounced – is dependent on the wider context of her life in much the same way as the idea that she is acting in a certain way – for example, that she is checkmating her opponent – is dependent on the wider context of her life.

This line of thought, which is associated primarily with a paper by the American philosopher Hilary Putnam, has been widely discussed in the recent literature, and various responses, by those sympathetic to the supervenience line of argument, have been proposed. The notes on further reading at the end of this chapter provide some references to this material.

(ii) My second point does not challenge any stage of the argument for this form of physicalism. It, rather, raises a doubt about the force of the conclusion.

Mental states, it is suggested, are 'nothing over and above' the physical states out of which they are composed. A suggestion of this form seems fairly central to the physicalist thought that: what *really – fundamentally* – exists is simply those elementary particles and their properties that are mentioned in the most basic physics. Assuming that we can go along with the 'supervenience' line of argument as far as it was taken in the previous section, what should we make of this suggestion?

David Lewis has said of the example of a picture of a face that the picture and its properties 'could go unmentioned in an inventory of what there is without thereby rendering that inventory incomplete' (Lewis, 1994, p. 413). He suggests that the same can be said of the mind and its states. But in what sense are these suggestions true? In the case of the painting, if one failed to mention the face and its features one would have failed to mention what is, for most of us most of the time, by far the most important thing about this object. It is true that if you gave me a large piece of paper, a set of paints, and a complete account of the arrangement of patches of colour on the canvas, I could, if I had the time, work out that what you were speaking of was a painting of a human face with that particular set of characteristics. And perhaps that provides *some* kind of grounds for saying that the face and its features are 'nothing over and above' the patches of paint on the canvas. But if one does say this it will be important to keep in mind precisely what that claim amounts to here.

And what of the claim that mental states are 'nothing over and above' the physical states out of which they are composed: that they 'could go unmentioned in an inventory of what there is without thereby rendering that inventory incomplete'. These claims would, perhaps, be acceptable if my aim in drawing up the inventory was to describe and explain the behaviour of the fundamental particles of physics. But if my aim is the more everyday one of telling my wife how the kids have been I will clearly have left out all the most important things if I do not mention how much they enjoyed the film, their disappointment that it was raining, and so on.

These remarks should not be read as a *denial* of claims of the 'nothing over and above' and 'complete inventory' variety. They are a reminder that when we come across them, or if we are tempted to make them ourselves, we should keep firmly in mind just what legitimate force they have in this context. My own view is that such claims mislead more than they illuminate. But that is not to reject the possibility that they can be read in a way such that they are true. It is simply to note that some of the normal connotations of such phrases may be quite out of place here.

6. The attractions of 'physicalism'

It is fairly widely assumed that anyone today who has her head firmly screwed on will subscribe to a doctrine that might be characterized as 'materialism', 'physicalism', or 'naturalism'. Much philosophical writing takes as its starting point a view described in some such terms, assuming that anyone who does not take such a doctrine to be *obviously* correct is inevitably outside the arena of serious debate. It is felt that, despite any difficulties of 'detail' in the defence of the particular forms of 'materialism' or 'physicalism' that I have discussed, it is clear that, once one has rejected Cartesian dualism, one is left with no alternative but to accept *some* version of these doctrines. That feeling is sometimes expressed in terms of the idea that the options that confront us are that *either* the mind is an immaterial soul in interaction with the brain *or* the mind is a material thing: the brain itself.

It is worth dwelling briefly on the terminology in which these discussions are conducted. The term 'materialism' has its natural home within a particular scientific world-view: one that, while it has been discarded by science itself, still has a powerful hold on the thinking of philosophically minded non-scientists. That scientific world-view is, very roughly, the view of seventeenth-century physics. Within that view, the fundamental constituents of nature are particles that can be thought of, more or less, on the model of minute billiard balls. They are, that is, solid, inert particles that interact with each other mechanistically: by way of motion in one particle being passed on to another through physical contact. A favourite model for such interaction was provided by the clock. (The mechanical, 'clockwork' clock, of course – not its modern digital replacements.) Everything, from the universe down to human beings (or 'the human body') and individual bodily organs, was represented as 'clockwork' systems of varying complexity. These systems were thought of as *mechanistic* in the sense that the behaviour of the whole flowed from the behaviour of minute particles of determinate shape, size, mass and solidity that interact with each other by physical contact, and with the kind of necessity that is involved in one billiard ball moving when it is struck by another.

Things are very different in the science – at least, in the physics – of the late twentieth century. The fundamental 'particles' (I am not even sure if that is the right word) of modern physics are not *material* entities in anything like the sense outlined. I am not sure that they have any shape, size, mass and solidity – or, at least, any *determinate* shape, size, mass and solidity; or, for that matter, any determinate location in space. With that, any attempt to picture their mutual interaction in terms of the physical contact and necessity that we find in the interactions of billiard balls is, I understand, quite inappropriate. Now whether one concludes that what is fundamental in modern physics is not *matter* – is not *material* entities – depends, of course, on precisely how one chooses to use the terms 'matter' and 'material'. What is clear is, as I said, that the ultimate elements of modern physics are not 'material' in anything like the sense in which the ultimate elements of seventeenth-century physics were material. This point is reflected in the fact that philosophers prefer now to speak of a doctrine, not of 'materialism', but of 'physicalism'. With this change in terminology we retain the idea that the world is fundamentally as it is described by physics, while abandoning the particular world-view of an earlier physics: the idea that what fundamentally exists is matter in motion.

My guess is that most readers of this book know little more than I do about the terms in which the contemporary physicist describes the phenomena that she studies. (Remember my embarrassed description of the process involved in water boiling!) Despite this, we perhaps retain the idea that, in some sense or other, how things are in the world is ultimately dictated by the laws governing the behaviour of the most elementary particles of which physics speaks. That idea is reflected in the pull that many feel towards 'physicalist' accounts of what a person is. I want now to make three points that may help to ease the force of that pull.

(i) In the first section of this chapter I presented an argument that purported to show that the current 'scientific world-view' may create difficulties for our normal understanding of ourselves, and of the ways in which our thoughts, feelings and so on may make a difference to what happens in the world; and in section 4 I suggested a way in which these difficulties might be overcome if we embraced a form of physicalism. The argument appealed to the idea that: 'everything that happens in the physical world has entirely physical causes'. Now in fact that is *not* an idea that is unambiguously endorsed in contemporary science; according to one central branch of physics – quantum physics – there are events in the physical world that happen without *any* cause. I want, however, to consider another, very different, form of doubt that we might have about the claim that 'everything that happens in the physical world has entirely physical causes'.

In the discussion of Descartes' view of the mind–body relation I noted the distinction between the following claims:

1. Everything that happens in the physical world has entirely physical causes.
2. Nothing that happens in the physical world involves a violation of the laws of physics.

Descartes, I noted, accepted the second but rejected the first. Now as it happens, his views about what was excluded by the laws of physics were not correct. But we should not let that blind us to the fact that the distinction he depended on is valid and important.

Consider an example. An extraordinary thing happens. I try to phone an old school friend with whom I have had no contact for five years. The line is engaged. As soon as I put the phone down it rings, and the school friend is on the line: my friend was trying to phone me at the very same time that I was trying to phone her. What was the cause of that? Well, there might be an answer to this question; for example, a mutual friend had just been mentioned in a news bulletin and we both wanted to find out more about what had happened. On the other hand, there might be no answer of that kind (or so most of us suppose). It was a coincidence.

To say that something was a 'coincidence' is, I take it, to say that there is no answer to the question: why did it happen? That is not to say that it involved a violation of the laws of physics. It is simply to say that it cannot be explained in terms of the laws of physics (or, if there be such, any other terms).

If the suggestion that 'everything that happens in the physical world has entirely physical causes' is the suggestion that 'everything that happens in the physical world can be explained entirely in terms of the laws of physics' then a consideration of coincidences makes it fairly clear that we have no reason to accept it. Consider now the movements of my body when I chop down a tree or give a lecture on the mind–body problem. Is it clear that these have entirely physical causes? Well, perhaps there is a fairly straightforward sense in which it is reasonable to suppose that each 'individual movement' of my body has entirely physical causes: the movement of my right arm through an arc of 30° is caused by the contraction of my arm muscles, which in turn is caused by … . But what of that complex bodily movement that is involved in a single swing of the axe – a complex movement that involves my arms, hips, legs, and more besides? From the fact that each of the individual movements of which this complex is composed can be explained entirely in terms of prior physiological events that caused it, it does not follow that the complex itself is caused by any prior physiological sequence. Of course, there *might* be an answer, in the physicist's or physiologist's terms, to the question: why did all of these individual physiological chains of events come together in just this way to produce a complex bodily movement of just this kind? (As there *might* be an answer to the question: why did my friend try to phone me at the very same time as I tried to phone her?) But there is, I take it, no reason to assume that there *must* be such an answer.

In connection with this example, I suggested, in the first section of this chapter, that pressure towards some form of physicalism comes from the idea that: 'the causes of the tree coming down are to be found entirely in the realm of the micro-entities of which physics speaks'. That idea seemed to leave no place for the claim that Jones' desire that it should come down had an essential role to play in its coming down – *unless* we thought of the desire as being, in some sense, 'realized by' a certain state of the physical micro-world. But, without suggesting that there is any violation of the laws of physics, we can reject the above claim about the physical causation of the tree coming down. For the falling of the tree was brought about by the blows of the axe; and these, in turn, were brought about by the series of complex bodily movements that were involved in my swinging the axe. And we have agreed that there need be no explanation of the occurrence of this particular complex bodily movement in terms of the behaviour of the micro-entities of which physics speaks. In that case, we can, perhaps, leave room for the idea that my desire has an essential role to play in the situation without resorting to any physicalist understanding of what a desire is.

This, I should stress, is no more than a sketch of a first step in a possible line of argument. I do not suggest that it is at all obvious how the account might be spelled out in detail. (See the paper by Lowe in the Further Reading section for one possible line of development in this direction.)

(ii) In my characterization of the physicalist view I spoke of the idea that the 'fundamental causal work' goes on at the level of the elementary particles of which the physicist speaks. That, the physicalist will insist, is not to suggest that there is anything wrong with our normal explanations: for example, our explanation of why Jones chopped down the tree in terms of his desire to improve the view. It is simply to say that the causal processes referred to in our everyday explanations are, in some sense, reducible to, or explainable by, those that operate at the more basic level spoken of in physics. Something of this form must, it is suggested, be true if the harmony between the two systems of prediction and explanation is not to be a perpetual fluke.

Well, *something* of that form perhaps. But one will only suppose that the solution must be of just the form outlined if one supposes that one has given clear sense to the phrase 'fundamental causal work'. We are, I think, tempted – or (to avoid possible offence!) perhaps I should say just that *I* am tempted – by very crude pictures here. We think, first, that when we observe one billiard ball colliding with, and propelling into motion, a second billiard ball we are observing *real* necessity: that we see why the second ball moves – see that it *has* to move – in a way in which we don't see why a magnet moves when another is placed close by it, or why water turns to steam when it is heated. And second, reflecting the hold on our thinking of seventeenth-century physics, we imagine that science reveals the *necessity* of the latter cases by showing that the magnets and water are composed of little – very little! – billiard balls bashing into each other. For example, the heat of the flame is really lots of tiny billiard balls rushing around at enormous speed; these collide with the billiard balls of which the water is composed so making them rush around much faster than they were before, until they eventually take off from the surface of the water.

Now there may be *some* sense in which that is the story that the scientist tells. But it is not clear that anything like that is going to have much application to the magnets. And, more important, there can be little doubt that as we move to deeper levels – as we move to the ever more fundamental particles of which today's physicist speaks – the billiard ball model rapidly becomes utterly inappropriate. Now if we can bring ourselves fully to acknowledge this (and I suspect that is quite a tricky business) then our sense that by moving to these 'deeper' levels we are discovering the real glue that holds the whole show together may begin to dissolve. For our idea of 'the real glue' – our idea of the 'necessity' at work – was derived from a model – that of the billiard balls – which has no application at this level.

The aim of these remarks is not to step on any scientists' toes. It is simply to raise a doubt about a certain 'metaphysical' picture that we are tempted to impose on popular accounts of the discoveries of science. Our image of where the 'fundamental causal work' is being done – the guys in the boiler room on which everything else rides piggy-back – may be tainted with serious muddle. In so far as that is so, we should not, perhaps, take it for granted that the 'harmony between the two systems of prediction and explanation' of which I have spoken *must* be understood in the terms suggested by physicalism.

(iii) Finally, I want to raise another very tentative doubt about the general metaphysical picture that drives much of the recent discussion of 'the place of mental states in the physical world'.

I earlier quoted Kim's formulation of the 'metaphysical conviction' that underlies physicalism: 'ultimately the world – at least, the physical world – is the way it is because the micro-world is the way it is'. But what exactly constitutes a feature of the micro-world? For example, does the fact that this collection of hydrogen atoms, at this particular instant, fills a spherical volume of space of 30 inches diameter constitute a feature of the micro-world? Presumably it does. At any rate, there are all kinds of phenomena that we will never be able to explain without reference to facts such as this: facts about the spatial relationships between the micro-entities of which the physicist speaks. For example, if you want to explain why the table with a rotten leg fell over you are going to have to speak of the particular collection of atoms of which a certain portion of one of its legs is composed: a portion 3 inches long, 2 inches in diameter, related in a particular way to the other micro-entities that constitute the table.

So if we are to accept the claim that 'ultimately the world... is the way it is because the micro-world is the way it is' it had better be the case that a description of the arrangement of micro-particles in a particular macro-volume of space can count as a 'description of the micro-world'. But having said that, how exactly are we to understand the contrast between 'how the macro-world is' and 'how the micro-world is'? We are asked to accept that the explanation of things being as they are in the normal world of our experience – the world of standard-sized objects – is ultimately to be found in a quite different world – a world of particles of a scale that is quite inaccessible to unaided human sense experience. The suggestion may create an eerie feeling. But before we are too unnerved we should be quite clear that we have given sense to the unsettling claim. A doubt about that arises, I have suggested, from the fact that in speaking of the 'micro-world' we have to speak of what are fairly unambiguously characteristics of the world of standard-sized objects.

I should stress that I do not suggest that any of these points amounts to a 'refutation of physicalism'. Points of this kind have been extensively discussed in the literature, and responses – of a kind that merit careful consideration – have been proposed. Further, some of these points that I have made in this and the previous section might be read, not as a 'demonstration of the falsity of physicalism', but as a demonstration that physicalism does not have the objectionable consequences some have supposed. Of course, much turns here on precisely what one means by the term 'physicalism'. My suspicion is that, at the end of the day, the issue might be not so much one of whether 'physicalism is true or false', as one of whether the language of physicalism is helpful and illuminating. And, for reasons that will be touched on in our consideration of freedom, my own view is that, on balance, it is not.

Further reading

Little of the literature on these themes is very accessible. One of the most important contributors to the discussion is Jaegwon Kim. His influential papers on these themes are collected in his book *Supervenience and Mind*; the paper 'Epiphenomenalism and Supervenient Causation' is particularly important. Chapters 6, 8 and 9 of Kim's *Philosophy of Mind* contain a more accessible defence of the kind of supervenience discussed in this chapter.

In Samuel Guttenplan (ed.), *A Companion to the Philosophy of Mind*, the entries on 'supervenience', 'Lewis, David: Reduction of Mind', 'physicalism (1)' and 'physicalism (2)' are helpful. Frank Jackson and Philip Pettit, 'Causation in the Philosophy of Mind' offers an interesting approach to the problem that motivates views discussed in this and the previous chapter.

The first of the two 'doubts' that I raise in section 5 is associated in particular with Hilary Putnam's 'The Meaning of "Meaning"'. It is usefully discussed in Kim's *Philosophy of Mind*, pp. 193–207.

In their paper 'There is No Question of Physicalism' Tim Crane and D.H. Mellor argue that it is not possible to give an explanation of what the term 'physical' means in a way such that the question of 'physicalism' can even arise; a related view is defended in Michael Tye, 'Naturalism and the Mental'. The paper by Crane and Mellor provoked a useful response by Philip Pettit in 'A Definition of Physicalism'. Crane replied to this in 'Reply to Pettit'.

In his paper 'The Causal Autonomy of the Mental', E.J. Lowe raises difficulties for one form of physicalism and presents considerations that are closely related to those discussed under point (i) in section 6 of this chapter.

Much of the discussion in this area turns on questions about the relations between explanations that we offer in different areas of our thought; and, in particular, on questions about the sense in which the explanations offered in physics might be said to be 'fundamental'. Interesting discussions of these more general questions can be found in J.A. Fodor, 'Special Sciences', and John Dupré, *The Disorder of Things*.

7
Human Beings

1. The mind, the body and the human being

In Chapter 5 we considered a standard argument for a thesis that might be formulated in this way: the mind, that which is the real subject of thoughts, emotions and sensations, is simply a physical organ of the body – namely, the brain. Now as I stressed, to knock down an argument for the mind–brain identity thesis is not itself to knock down the mind–brain identity thesis; still less is it to knock down the other varieties of physicalism that are now on offer. And many will, I suspect, feel that nothing that was said in Chapters 5 and 6 is a very serious threat to materialist thinking. At most, the considerations presented suggest that the argument may need a bit of patching up (and I know people who will feel that even this is conceding far too much!) This feeling springs in part, I think, from the idea that the options for an account of what a person is are exhausted by, on the one hand, dualism and, on the other, some version of the thesis that the mind is the brain. If we simply take this for granted we are – given the position that the sciences now have in our culture and the popular perception of what has been achieved by science – almost bound to reach the conclusion that the truth must be found in *some* form of the latter thesis.

I should stress here that I do not believe that the physicalist *has* to commit herself to any thesis that could be usefully formulated as the claim that 'the mind is the brain'. Nor do I believe that she has to commit herself to the various ideas that I will link with that claim in this section. My aim in this section, as in the previous two chapters, is not to 'prove the falsity of physicalism'. It is, rather, to cast doubt on one cluster of ideas that, I suspect, lies at the roots of much physicalist thinking.

To see that it is possible that dualism and the mind–brain identity thesis do not exhaust the options, it will be helpful to return to the distinction that I drew between three different strands in the Cartesian account. These can be summarized in this way:

1. It is through my experience of *myself* that I grasp what a person is; and through my experience of my own thoughts, emotions and sensations that I grasp what *these* are.
2. The real person is something other than the human being that we actually see when we 'meet another person'. The real person is 'the mind': a non-material entity that is causally connected with the brain.
3. The extended, tangible thing – the 'human body' – that I see when I look at another human being is, in itself, a 'physical object', no different in fundamental kind from any other.

The functionalist version of materialism involves a rejection of the first of these assumptions. It involves, too, a rejection of the second half of assumption 2. But assumption 3 and the first half of assumption 2 appear to be common to traditional dualism and at least some of the recent materialist alternatives. If there is some way in which these might be questioned then there may, perhaps, be room for some alternative to the two broad options considered so far.

Consider the third assumption. My presentation of it raises some difficulty as it is not completely clear what is involved in the claim that something is a 'physical object'; or, closely linked with that, what Descartes is committing himself to when he speaks of the human body as a 'machine'. If the claim is simply that what I see when I look at another human being is an extended, tangible thing then it can hardly be disputed. But suppose that what is being claimed is, in part, this: a full description of what we see when we see another human being can be given entirely in 'physical' terms; that is to say, in terms of the language employed by the natural (the physical) sciences. (Remember David Lewis' suggestion that the picture and its properties 'could go unmentioned in an inventory of what there is without thereby rendering that inventory incomplete'.) Now *this* claim – which is, perhaps, not always clearly distinguished from the first – is much more controversial. For, as I have stressed, our descriptions of the 'behaviour' of another are normally in terms of the following kinds: 'He smiled while he waved goodbye', 'He gave her an angry glance', 'She checkmated him', 'She voted for the motion'. With that, it is generally in terms such as these that we 'see' another's behaviour. We spontaneously respond to what we see *as to* a smile or an angry glance; and asked to describe another's behaviour in terms other than these – in terms, for example, of the 'ways in which her body moved' – we would generally find ourselves struggling. We would find ourselves struggling because it is not as described in these other terms – it is not as movements of a body – that another's behaviour is generally of interest to us.

The terms in which we normally understand the 'behaviour' of another are *not* those of the natural sciences. The language of 'smiles' and 'angry glances' has no place in physics as it is normally understood. In what sense, then, can it be said that: a proper description of what we see when we see another human being can be given entirely in terms of the language employed by the natural sciences?

Consider now the characterization of a 'naturalistic', or 'physicalist', view offered in a recent introduction to the philosophy of mind. Smith and Jones describe such a view as being one that 'invokes no entities unrecognised by the natural sciences' (Smith and Jones, 1986, p. 162). Now it is tempting to take the central philosophical question about the notion of a person – that which divides the dualist from the materialist – to be this: in explaining the 'behaviour' of human beings, do we need to invoke any 'entities unrecognised by the natural sciences'? But this understanding of the issue completely bypasses the question of whether in *describing* the behaviour of human beings we need to invoke 'entities unrecognised by the natural sciences'. If, as I have suggested, we do, then we can reject dualism without suggesting that a human being can be adequately characterized entirely in terms drawn from the natural sciences.

This brings us to the other assumption that, I suggested, may be shared by traditional dualism and certain recent materialist alternatives to it: the assumption that the real person is something other than the human being that we actually see when we 'meet another person'. We might express the point here in this way. The mind–brain identity thesis simply takes over the mind/body distinction as it is understood by Descartes. The 'mind' is that part of the person in which thought, emotion, sensation and so on take place; such states and activities are states and activities of 'the mind'. The 'body' is all the rest: the organic, but 'mechanical', part of the person, which can be adequately characterized in the terms of the natural sciences. With that, 'the body' – that is, what we see when we look at another human being – is clearly not the entity that feels pain, gets angry, and so on. The dispute between the views is a dispute about whether 'the mind' – understood as the bit that *does* feel pain, get angry or think about philosophy – is just another material object or whether it is an entity of a quite different, non-material, kind.

That understanding of the 'mind'/'body' division is so deeply entrenched in the philosophical study of people that it is embalmed in the title of that area of study: 'the philosophy of mind'. It is so deeply entrenched that discussion of these issues, and not only by those who call themselves 'philosophers', are conducted in terms of a contrast between 'mental' and 'physical' characteristics which, from the point of view of our everyday, unselfconscious, understanding is quite bizarre. Thus, Armstrong writes: 'We say that we have a pain in the hand. The *sensation* of pain can hardly be in the hand, for sensations are in minds and the hand is not part of the mind' (Armstrong, 1984, p. 182). Armstrong asserts, without any kind of defence, that 'sensations are in minds'. Yet in our normal speech we draw a sharp *contrast* between 'physical' and 'mental' pains. And if, on complaining to my doctor of a pain in my back, she informed me that the pain was all in my mind I might be puzzled or I might be irritated, but I would certainly not take her to be telling me something that is obviously true.

This appeal to our normal speech does not show that Armstrong's conclusion – 'the sensation of pain is not in the hand' – is false. It does, however, show that he is going to have to say more if we are to see even the beginnings of a decent argument for this claim. Now it might be felt that this is not difficult to provide. Just look at a hand and ask yourself: is that the kind of thing that could feel pain – or, if this is different, the kind of thing in which there could be a pain? We will all, it might be suggested, find difficulty in this supposition when we reflect on it; and so we will be forced to concede that the real location of the sensation is somewhere else: in 'the mind'.

A materialist of Armstrong's variety cannot too happily appeal to this thought. For one who suggests that 'the mind' is the brain is committed to the view that the sensation is in the brain; and I suspect that most of us, confronted with such a lump of grey matter, would have as much difficulty, or more, in supposing that it was in pain (or that a pain was in it). In any case, the question with which I suggested Armstrong might attempt to nudge us in his direction needs to be handled more carefully. For in asking us to consider the *hand*, the question draws our attention away from the *human being* whose hand it is. Wittgenstein writes:

What sort of issue is: Is it the *body* that feels pain?—How is it to be decided? What makes it plausible to say that it is *not* the body?—Well, something like this: if someone has a pain in his hand, then the hand does not say so (unless it writes it) and one does not comfort the hand, but the sufferer: one looks into his face. (Wittgenstein, 1968, §286)

It is the *person*, the *human being*, that we normally speak of as being in pain: as feeling pain. Now if we ask of the human being 'Is *that* the kind of thing that could feel pain?' the answer seems clear: 'Certainly. That is just the kind of thing that could feel pain.' We will, then, no longer feel any pressure to conclude that what really feels the pain is something else – 'the mind' – that *lies behind* what we observe of the other.

Suppose, slightly differently, that we ask of a hand: 'Is that the kind of thing in which there could be a pain?' If one asks this question with one's attention concentrated fixedly on the hand one might hesitate. But if one remembers that the hand is the hand of a human being, and if one asks 'Could a human being feel a pain in this?' the answer again seems clear. Just look at a human being with a pain in her hand and any difficulty one might have felt evaporates.

2. 'An attitude towards a soul'

It will be helpful here to focus on a consideration that has surfaced at a number of points in our discussion: one that may be partly responsible for the pull of the dualist version of the mind/body contrast. In the above passage, and in many others, Wittgenstein gives a central place to ways in which we *respond* to – are concerned about – other human beings: ways which mark our thought of other people off from our thought about inanimate objects. We feel about and treat others – at least some others, some of the time – in a quite distinctive range of ways; and we think it appropriate to do so. What I have in mind here covers a wide range of phenomena. For example, in certain circumstances we think it appropriate to feel pity towards others, and to comfort them – when, that is, they are in pain. We feel gratitude or resentment towards others when they have acted in certain ways; that is to say, we mind how others treat us in a way in which we do not characteristically mind about the behaviour of inanimate objects and, perhaps, most animals. Closely connected with this is the way in which we mind how others, and especially some others, think of us; for example, another's anger can be disturbing, frightening, in a way that has nothing to do with a fear that he might physically assault

us: a tree's branches waving in the wind do not have the same significance for me as a man shaking his fist at me. All of this is connected in
various ways with the notion of respecting another. Think, for example, of the kind of contempt for another that might be expressed in my
complete indifference concerning her opinion of me, or in my complete indifference to the fact that her eyes are on me. Again, there are
limitations on the ways in which we generally think it appropriate to
treat others: limitations that might be summarized in terms of the idea
that it is not appropriate to *use* others. That is to say, certain forms of
treatment of another are not in place even in cases in which that treatment might be in her own best interests. Thus, sane adults are generally to be influenced by being given reasons to do or feel whatever
we judge that they should do or feel; they are not, except in extreme
circumstances, to be influenced by threats, drugs administered without
their knowledge, or lies.

This very incomplete list will serve to illustrate the forms of response
to others that I have in mind. Now something that may push someone
towards the kind of dualism outlined in the first chapter is, I think, an
idea of this form: unless the real person is something quite different in
kind from what we can see and touch, these attitudes would be out of
place; and, with that, the idea that, as we might express it, people have
a special kind of value would be undermined. The 'mind' or 'soul' is,
then, the non-material, value-conferring entity that lies behind the
observable human being.

The idea here is simply that our normal ways of thinking about each
other require the dualist picture. Nothing along these lines could do
anything to show that dualism is a correct account of what we are: that
there is such a thing as 'the soul'. Indeed, if one thinks of the soul in
this way one may well suspect that modern science has created serious
difficulties for the idea that there is any such thing. The psychologist
J.B. Watson writes 'No one has ever touched the soul, or seen one in a
test tube, or has in any way come into a relationship with it as he has
with other objects of his daily experience' (Watson and McDougall,
1928, p. 13). Further, one might feel, it is not simply that no one has
ever observed the soul directly. It seems increasingly clear that the
hypothesis that there is such a thing is not required to explain any of
the observed behaviour of human beings; at any rate, there appears to
be no reason to doubt that it is in principle possible to explain every
movement of the human body in physiological terms. This, of course,
is the thought that is central to the defences of materialism considered
in Chapters 5 and 6.

Thus, it is widely felt that modern science leaves no room for the idea of the soul. With this, it is sometimes felt that modern science demands a fundamental revision in our conception of the kind of value that people have, and so in our understanding of the kinds of attitude towards people that are appropriate. Very roughly speaking, it is felt that science has shown that the idea that there is some fundamental way in which we are marked off from the rest of nature must be abandoned. The differences are differences in complexity, not in kind. (We will consider in Chapter 9 an area of our thinking in which this idea has a particularly powerful hold: that which relates to the idea of 'human freedom'.)

It should be stressed that not all materialists draw these conclusions about what I have called 'the kind of value' that people have. I was, there, speaking as much of the popular perception of materialism as of the claims actually defended by its main exponents. What I wish to draw attention to here, however, is the fact that dualism and materialism – when it takes the form just outlined – share the following assumption:

> Talk about the 'soul' is talk about a non-material entity that some believe to be connected with the human body. Those attitudes that are expressive of our idea that people have a special kind of value are dependent on a belief in the existence of entities of this kind. Scientific investigation is relevant to the question of whether this belief is true.

The two views differ only over the question of what the scientific evidence suggests.

It might be felt that the use of the word 'only' in my last sentence is slightly absurd. What difference could be greater than this one? Well, from the point of view of another approach to our idea of the value of a human being, that difference does not appear to be of such great significance. This approach is encapsulated in the following remark: 'My attitude towards him is an attitude towards a soul. I am not of the *opinion* that he has a soul' (Wittgenstein, 1968, p. 178). In this remark Wittgenstein rejects the shared assumption of which I spoke. His point, in part, is that those attitudes that go with the idea of people as having a special kind of value are not dependent on a belief that is more fundamental than them: the belief that human beings have 'non-material minds' or 'souls'. Thus, no scientific evidence concerning the existence or non-existence of these supposed non-material entities is of any relevance to the question of whether the special attitudes that we have towards people are in place.

In Chapter 3 we considered the argument from analogy for 'the existence of other minds'. We might express the relationship of ideas presupposed by that approach in the following way:

> The special range of attitudes that I have towards another human being is dependent on (requires the underpinning of) a belief that this is a being of a kind that has thoughts, emotions, sensations and so on; and that belief stands in need of justification in terms of analogies between the other's body and behaviour and my own.

Now in rejecting the idea that I am 'of the *opinion* that he has a soul' Wittgenstein is, I think, rejecting both steps in this approach. The special range of attitudes that I have towards other human beings does not require the underpinning of some *belief* that I hold about them; and, with that, does not stand in need of justification in terms of analogies with myself. The attitudes, we might say, are what is most basic in my relation to another. I respond to what I see – to the *human being* – with pity, resentment, gratitude and so on: that is, in ways that mark off my thoughts and feelings about others from my thoughts and feelings about trees or cars.

Now it might be objected that Wittgenstein's view is, at this point, radically unphilosophical. For isn't it of the essence of philosophy to demand *justifications* – *reasons* – for what, in everyday life, we simply take for granted? Well, Wittgenstein suggests that we need radically to revise our conception of the task of philosophy. But we need not pursue that beyond noting a point on which he often insists: all justifications come to an end somewhere (Wittgenstein, 1968, §217 and §485). A fundamental difference between different philosophical outlooks lies in their differing views about just *where* it is no longer appropriate to ask for further justifications. In the context that is our immediate concern Wittgenstein suggests that we reach this point a stage earlier than is assumed by proponents of the argument from analogy. We should not assume that we need a justification – in terms of some theory about the causes of the behaviour that we observe – for the attitude towards other human beings that is reflected in our responses to their tears, smiles and so on.

This is not to deny that there might be particular cases in which there is room for a justification for thinking that the familiar attitudes are in place. Consider a case, for example, in which someone assumes, wrongly, that the histrionics of her actress friend are simply part of a rehearsal for a play; we might need to offer reasons for thinking that this is for real, and so that the normal range of attitudes is in place. The force of Wittgenstein's point can be brought out by contrasting the case of this person with someone who characteristically, with no special reason, shows no acknowledgement in her words, feelings or behaviour of the pain, grief, joy, or whatever that we can see in those with whom she is confronted. To insist that we need a *justification* for our normal beliefs and feelings when confronted with someone who, as we would say, is 'in obvious pain' or 'grief' is to insist that: in the absence of such a justification the appropriate, the philosophical, the clear-thinking, response is one of doubt or indifference. But why on earth should we accept *that*?

3. The object of pity

With this in mind, we can return to what I suggested were two strands of Cartesian thinking that may be carried over in at least some versions of materialism. These were, first, the idea that the real person is 'the mind' – that is, something other than the human being that we actually see when we 'meet another person' – and, second, the idea that the extended, tangible thing – the 'human body' – that I see when I look at another human being is, in itself, a 'physical object', no different in fundamental kind from any other.

I have, at many points in this book, stressed that the language in which we describe the behaviour of ourselves and others is not, characteristically, the language of physics; nor, if this is different, is it the language of geometrical movements of matter in space. This is a reflection of the fact that we do not, at the most primitive level, 'see' others as simply mechanical systems. As I expressed the matter in Chapter 4, I *see* the joy in another's face, I *see* the anger in the other's eyes, I *see* people laughing at jokes and writhing in agony, and so on. I do not see flesh – 'a body' – moving in certain ways, and on the basis of this 'infer' that there is here a joyful person, or 'interpret' this as a person in pain. I *see* the joy in her face. I *see* the pain in her grimaces and hear it in her cries. I see and hear these things in the sense that I respond to her with, for example, a smile, or with pity. The language in which we describe what we see is an expression of these responses to others: responses that, Wittgenstein has suggested, we should not regard as standing in need of any general justification.

In what sense, then, can it be said that the extended, tangible being that I see when I look at another human being is, in itself, a 'physical object', no different in fundamental kind from any other? Well, we can agree that we can, with considerable effort and for limited periods, see the other in that way. Wittgenstein tries to capture the experience (Wittgenstein, 1968, §420). He compares it with the way in which one might see the cross-pieces of a window as a swastika; though an example that is in some ways more illuminating might be that of seeing some object – say a tree outside your window – as a clever imitation made out of paper or plastic. (I hope you understand what I am speaking about here sufficiently well to give it a shot.) But, as I hope the analogy brings out, the fact that one *can* see, and describe, another in this way does not at all show that that is the way in which the other *is to be seen*, and *is to be described*. It does not show that when we see the other in that way we see her as she *really* is. And so we cannot argue:

> What I actually *see* when I am confronted with another human being is a physical object, no different in kind, but only in complexity, from any other. So my distinctive responses towards others – responses of pity, resentment, respect, and so on – can only be in place in so far as the real person is something distinct from that which I actually see.

For if by the term 'physical object' we mean 'object of a kind such that responses like this are not in place' then we do not need to accept that what we see of others is 'simply a complex physical object'. And if by the term 'physical object' we mean 'thing of a kind that has weight, height, and so on' then we do not need to accept that no 'physical object' can be an appropriate object of such responses.

Wittgenstein goes further. He writes: '[O]nly of a living human being and what resembles (behaves like) a living human being can one say: it has sensations; it sees; is blind; hears; is deaf; is conscious or unconscious' (Wittgenstein, 1968, §281). It is not simply that we do not *have* to think that the person – what really gets angry, feels pain, and so on – is something other than the living human being: for example, a brain or a 'non-material mind'. A living human being – or what resembles one – is the only *possible* candidate for that position.

We can, perhaps, see why he takes this view when we reflect on his suggestion that it is my *attitude* towards her that is what is most basic in my relation to another. 'Thinking of another as a person' is not some 'internal state' that underlies the attitude. It is *in* the ways in which I respond to the other with pity, gratitude, joy, envy and so on that we see the sense in which I think of another person as a being quite different in kind from, say, a stone. Now these ways in which

I respond are, at least in many cases, closely bound up with the particular bodily form of the other. In a passage quoted earlier Wittgenstein writes: 'one does not comfort the hand, but the sufferer: one looks into his face'. I look into his face, into his eyes, with sympathy. In a slightly different way, my horror at another's suffering may be inseparable from a distress in seeing her contorted face and hearing her cries. Again, it may not be possible to characterize the pleasure that I take in another's joy without speaking of my desire to see her joyful face, to hear her laughter, and, perhaps, to laugh with her. My fear of another's anger might be seen most directly in my keeping him at a safe distance, and, more interestingly, in my attempts to avoid his gaze.

I hope that this very limited range of examples is at least sufficient to suggest a possible difficulty in the supposition that I might feel about, and respond to, something that lacks anything like the human form in just the ways that are characteristic of my responses to a human being: to suggest, that is, a possible difficulty in the supposition that I might have towards a stone – or, for that matter, a brain or a 'non-material mind' – what Wittgenstein speaks of as 'an attitude towards a soul'. In so far as they do that, they show that it is far from clear what it would be to think of something other than a human being – or what resembles a human being – as a *person*.

The conclusion of my last three sections might be expressed in this way. Philosophers, and perhaps others, go wrong when they think that what needs to be investigated is the nature of 'the mind'. I do not say this because I think it is clear that the idea of a 'mind' is a fiction. I say it because the aim of philosophers who have worked on what is traditionally known as 'the philosophy of mind' has been, at least in part, to investigate the nature of that part of the human being – namely, 'the mind' – that is fundamental to our being the particular kind of beings that we are. As we might express it: the aim has been to investigate the nature of that part of the human being that is the real subject of thoughts, emotions, sensations and so on. In opposition to this, I have suggested that it is the *human being herself* – not some part of her, or something that inhabits, and animates, her body – that thinks, gets angry, feels pain, and so on; and, closely linked with that, it is the *human being* that we pity, love or fear.

4. 'Souls', human beings and animals

I spoke of a range of responses that are expressive of the idea that people have a special kind of value. This range of responses is a pretty mixed bag. It is, for example, one thing to refrain from hurting some-one, and quite another to show her the specific kind of respect that we may show for someone in the way we dispose of her dead body. Now the dualist way of thinking about the soul has, I think, a tendency to flatten out these differences. For the Cartesian dualist there is, one might say, one clean divide in the world: a being either has a 'soul' or it does not. This came out in the fact that when I was speaking of dualism I used the terms 'mind' and 'soul' interchangeably. Now these terms have rather different connotations in normal speech; the term 'soul' has connotations of a more distinctly religious or spiritual character. Within dualism, however, such distinctions tend to disappear. The thing that thinks, has sensations and so on is the immaterial entity that is connected with the body. Thus, as soon as we grant that something has sensations – that it has a 'mind' in that sense – we are allowing that it has what is crucial to the possession of value of all kinds. (Descartes sometimes seems to deny that animals think or have sensations on the grounds that to suggest that they do would commit us to the view, which he judged to be absurd, that they have 'immortal souls'.)

Once we give up the idea that what is crucial to the possession of value is the presence of an entity of a special kind, it becomes easier to acknowledge distinctions within this range of responses. Thus, the atti-tude that most have towards cows or dogs is quite different from that which we have towards cars. Yet it is also quite different from the atti-tude most of us have towards people. For example, the kind of respect involved in the idea that there are limitations on how we may treat other people, even for their own good, is, for most of us, significantly less clearly marked in our thought about animals. One instance of this is the fact that most of us would 'put a cow out of its misery' by killing it very much more readily than we would a person; another, and rather different, illustration is to be found in the fact that many of us eat cows. Further, there are, of course, radical differences in our attitudes towards different kinds of animal: few in our society would shoot a dog in quite the casual way in which we swat a fly. Now there is, of course, plenty of room for argument as to whether the attitude most of us have towards animals in general, and towards particular species of animal, is at all what it should be. My point is simply that it is far from obvious that clear thinking about these issues is helped by a dualist picture that suggests that 'having a mind/soul' – being a proper object of certain forms of respect – is an all-or-nothing matter; so that one who insists that we should take the suffering of cows more seriously than we do is committed to the view that we ought to give them funerals.

The remarks in my last paragraph are closely connected with the fact that most of us would not speak of 'souls' in connection with cows or dogs. My attitude towards a cow is not an attitude towards a soul. I am not in fact sure that *my* attitude towards a person is an attitude towards a soul. While I believe that other people make a range of distinctive and enormously important demands on us, a protest against a violation of these demands, a protest against the lack of concern or respect with which a particular group is being treated, might be made in terms of a reminder that 'These are human beings!' I suspect that many others in our society today think roughly as I do here. They have no great use for the word 'soul', and do not think of human beings as having just the kind of value that is traditionally associated with that term.

The term does, as I said, have its natural place within a, broadly speaking, religious context, and one who uses it would fairly certainly make demands on our attitude towards each other that go beyond what is, perhaps, now the norm in this society. I will not try to say anything about what these demands might be, beyond noting what may already have struck you as a glaring gap in my discussion. Is not the notion of the soul crucially bound up with the idea that we live on after the death of the body? Further, is it not clear that that dimension of our thought about the soul can only be accommodated within the approach associated with Descartes, and not within that which derives from Wittgenstein? Of course, we might accept that, and argue that the latter approach does, nevertheless, rescue all that can be rescued of traditional talk of 'the soul'. I am not myself convinced that we should accept it, but that is not a line of argument that can be developed here. The next chapter will, however, have a direct, if largely negative, bearing on certain ways in which we might be inclined to picture 'life after the death of the body'.

5. Could a machine think?

An intense interdisciplinary debate over the last fifty years or so has focused on the idea of 'artificial intelligence'. The issue at the centre of this debate is sometimes formulated in terms of the question 'Could a machine think?', or 'Could a machine be a person?' Further, those questions are widely felt to bear directly on our understanding of what *we* are: a supposed bearing that is neatly articulated in such lurid questions as 'Is the brain's mind a computer program?' (Searle, 1990, p. 20). The discussion of these issues is often highly technical, and is, as one might expect, often closely linked with the kinds of view considered in the previous two chapters. I want, however, briefly to consider one, completely untechnical, aspect of the discussion: an aspect that bears more closely on the concerns of the present chapter.

In an article published in 1950, the mathematical logician Alan Turing suggested that the best way of approaching the question 'Could a machine think?' is in terms of what he called the 'imitation game'. Suppose that we built a computer that answers questions typed into a console. Of course, we already have such computers of various levels of sophistication. But suppose that we had – what we do not now have – a computer that could answer any question that we asked just as a human being might answer it: that is to say, in a way such that one could not tell from the answers that this was not a human being. Suppose, for example, that you are in electronic communication, through a console, with a person and with a computer. We can call one of them 'Fred' and the other 'Jack'; but you have not been told whether it is Fred or Jack that is the computer. You can ask Fred and Jack any questions that you want, and must try to work out from their answers which is the human being and which the computer. Turing suggested that we should say that we have produced a thinking machine if we have produced a machine that we are unable, however close our questioning, to distinguish from a human being in this way. (Note: the machine has *not* been programmed for truthfulness. That would make the questioner's task too easy!)

Turing suggested that there is no reason to suppose that there could not be a mechanical device that passes this test. Others have raised doubts about that. The following example gives some flavour of the character of these doubts:

> A rookie bus driver, suspended for failing to do the right thing when a girl suffered a heart attack on his bus, was following overly strict rules that prohibit drivers from leaving their routes without permission, a union official said yesterday. 'If the blame has to be put anywhere, put it on the rules that those people have to follow' [said the official]. [A spokesman for the bus company defending the rules argued]: 'You give them a little leeway, and where does it end up?' (*Arizona Daily Star*, 31 May 1986. Quoted: Crane, 1995, p. 119)

Such examples, it is suggested, bring out that the behaviour of an intelligent human being could never be captured in a set of rules that might be programmed into a machine. Now it might be objected that the trouble in the above case was simply that the rules were too simple: that there is no difficulty in principle in formulating a set of rules that would be a symbolic representation of human intelligence. To this, others have replied that no refinements in the rules, however complex, could ever dictate the correct response – the intelligent human being's response – in every possible situation: what is needed is 'the background of common sense that adult human beings have by virtue of having bodies, interacting skilfully with the material world, and being trained in a culture' (Dreyfus, 1992, p. 3).

Rather than pursuing that line of argument, however, I want to consider a different form of objection to the Turing test: an objection that suggests that even if there could be a mechanical device that passes the test, that would not be sufficient grounds for the claim that there could be a mechanical device that thinks. The objection, which has become known as the Chinese room argument, was developed by the philosopher, John Searle:

> Imagine that I, a non-Chinese speaker, am locked in a room with a lot of Chinese symbols in boxes. I am given an instruction book in English for matching Chinese symbols with other Chinese symbols and for giving back bunches of Chinese symbols in response to bunches of Chinese symbols put into the room through a small window. Unknown to me, the symbols put in through the window are called questions. The symbols I give back are called answers to the questions. … imagine that I get so good at shuffling the symbols, and the programmers get so good at writing the program, that eventually my 'answers' to the 'questions' are indistinguishable from those of a native Chinese speaker. I pass the Turing test for understanding Chinese. But all the same, I don't understand a word of Chinese. (Searle, 1994, p. 546)

Searle concludes that what is relevant to the question of whether something understands Chinese (or thinks, has beliefs, has sensations, is conscious, and so on) is not simply, as Turing assumes, that, given a certain input, it produces the 'correct' output. It is also crucial that the process – the internal mechanism – by which the output is produced is of a certain kind. In the case of human beings this process is *biologically* based; and we know that human beings think. That does not show that *only* biological systems are capable of thought. But it does, according to Searle, bring out that the internal workings of a system – not simply its input and output – are crucial to the question of whether that system thinks.

But both Turing's test and Searle's response to it contain a bias of which we should, I think, be suspicious. Turing suggested that his approach to the issue 'has the advantage of drawing a fairly sharp line between the physical and the intellectual capacities of a man' (Turing, 1950, p. 434). The line is drawn by virtue of the fact that the interrogator cannot see, touch or hear that with which she is in communication. Now there is, of course, *some* kind of line to be drawn between 'physical' and 'intellectual' capacities: there is, for example, the person who is a good runner but hopeless at mental arithmetic. We might, however, begin to wonder whether the line is quite as sharp as Turing suggests, or whether it is to be drawn in quite the way that he suggests, when we ask on which side of it the concert pianist or the skilled cabinet maker falls. We might press this point further by asking whether we really have been offered sufficient reason for giving to *verbal* behaviour the kind of priority Turing gives it. Consider, for example, a sharply contrasting approach suggested by Wittgenstein in the following passage:

> Of course we cannot separate his 'thinking' from his activity. For the thinking is not an accompaniment of the work, any more than of thoughtful speech.
>
> Were we to see creatures at work whose *rhythm* of work, play of expression etc. was like our own, but for their not *speaking*, perhaps in that case we should say that they thought, considered, made decisions. For there would be a *great deal* there corresponding to the action of ordinary humans. (Wittgenstein, 1967, §§101–2)

Both Turing and Searle are operating with a radical 'mind'/'body' contrast. They are assuming, that is, that the fact that we are beings of a particular bodily form – beings of the human form – who act in the world is quite irrelevant to the idea that we are beings who think. Indeed, the assumption is more radical than that way of putting it suggests. For when I said, in my presentation of Searle's view, that 'we know that human beings think' there was some misrepresentation of his position. For, according to Searle, it is not human beings that think, but their *brains*. The assumption that it is the brain that thinks – as it is the heart that pumps blood – is one that is seen again and again in discussions of these issues. It is an assumption that is reflected, in a quite unselfconscious way, in many popular expositions of recent scientific research on human thought and cognition. Now that research makes it clear, no doubt, that there is *some* kind of close connection between thought and what takes place in the brain; but that does not, by itself, show that it is brains, rather than human beings, that think. Of course, there could still be something to be said for the assumption. (Though I, as you might guess, have my doubts!) But it is important that one does not lose a sense of the strangeness of that way of speaking: that one does not uncritically swallow the assumption along with the science.

If one does not accept the assumption, if one holds that the person is the *human being*, and that there is a link – of roughly the form suggested by Wittgenstein – between the idea of a creature as 'thinking' and that creature's *behaviour*, then one will maintain that the way in which Turing and Searle set up the issue of 'artificial intelligence' is misconceived. To express the point in their terms: one will maintain that, in their images of messages through consoles or notes through windows, they offer us a seriously impoverished understanding of the 'input' and 'output' that is relevant to the claim that some creature is thinking. That, in itself, will not tell us on which side we should come down in the dispute between them. It will, however, cast that dispute in a very different light.

Further reading

This chapter draws heavily on the work of Wittgenstein and those influenced by him. Particularly relevant passages in Wittgenstein's own writings are *Philosophical Investigations* §§281–8, §§412–27, Part II sections iv and v; and *Zettel* §§218–25, §§528–74. Two accessible discussions that are strongly influenced by Wittgenstein, and that give a central place to his idea of 'an attitude towards a soul', are Ilham Dilman, *Love and Human Separateness* (see especially chapters 2, 3, 5 and 8), and Ben Tilghman, *The View From Eternity*, chapter 5. Very important, but more difficult, discussions of Wittgenstein's approach to these issues can be found in John Cook, 'Human Beings', in Peter Winch (ed.), *Studies in the Philosophy of Wittgenstein*, and in Peter Winch, ' "Eine Einstellung Zur Seele" ', in his *Trying to Make Sense*. Chapters 4 and 8 of Fergus Kerr, *Theology After Wittgenstein* contain relevant, interesting, and quite accessible discussions. I discuss these issues at greater length in my *Other Human Beings* (see especially chapters 1, 3, 5 and 6).

The idea that that 'the mind' is a part of the person – the part in which thoughts, emotions, and so on occur – is usefully criticized in Roger Squires, 'On One's Mind'. Another useful paper in which, among other things, he discusses the notion of a 'physical object' is Roger Squires, 'Zombies v Materialists'.

Questions about our relations with non-human creatures are discussed in illuminating terms, within a Wittgensteinian framework, in Cora Diamond, 'Eating Meat and Eating People', in her *The Realistic Spirit*. Diamond's discussion brings out the close connection between Wittgenstein's views and a range of ethical issues. Those connections are also prominent in her paper 'The Importance of Being Human'. For very different approaches, ones that argue, on ethical grounds, that we must maintain a fundamental distinction between the idea of a person and the idea of a human being, see Michael Tooley, 'Abortion and Infanticide', and Peter Singer, *Animal Liberation*.

The contemporary discussion of thinking machines takes off from A.M. Turing, 'Computing Machinery and Intelligence'. John Searle presents his Chinese room argument in a number of places; see, for example, John Searle, *Minds, Brains and Science*. For an approach to these issues with a Wittgensteinian flavour see Hubert L. Dreyfus, *What Computers Still Can't Do*, especially Part II. For an introductory text that offers a very different approach see Tim Crane, *The Mechanical Mind*.

8
The Identity of the Self

1. Thoughts and thinkers

The turning point in Descartes' thinking – the point at which he finds that he can put a stop to the doubt induced by the hypothesis of the malignant demon – is that at which he turns to his knowledge of his own existence and of the contents of his own mind. He suggests that in his conviction that he is 'thinking', and that he exists, he encounters certainties about which there is no possibility that he could be mistaken.

But it is not completely clear how Descartes understands the relationship between his claim 'I think' and his claim 'I am'. Suppose, for example, that he was confronted with the following thought:

> For my part, when I enter most intimately into what I call *myself*, I always stumble on some particular perception or other, of heat or cold, light or shade, love or hatred, pain or pleasure. I never can catch *myself* at any time without a perception, and never can observe any thing but the perception. (Hume, 1739, pp. 301–2)

These are the words of the Scottish philosopher David Hume (1711–76), writing one hundred years after Descartes produced his *Meditations*. Now it is possible that Descartes would accept Hume's observation; it is possible that he would accept that what he is immediately aware of in an indubitable way is simply a series of thoughts, emotions, sensations and so on. He might accept this, but add that where there are thoughts there *must* be a thinker. Indeed, this is precisely the way in which he presents the matter in the following passage:

> … it must be remarked, as a matter that is highly manifest by the natural light, that to nothing no affections or qualities belong; and,

accordingly, that where we observe certain affections, there a thing or substance to which these pertain, is necessarily found.

He suggests that it follows that:

> ... there is no occasion on which we know anything whatever when we are not at the same time led with much greater certainty to the knowledge of our own mind. (Descartes, 1644, pp. 168–9)

Descartes is arguing that it is 'highly manifest by the natural light' that 'thinking' is what he calls an 'affection': that is to say, that it is an occurrence of a kind that can only exist in so far as there is something that does it, or has it. An analogy would be the way in which it is clear that there can be no occurrence of the kind 'a running of a race' unless there are *people* (or some other creatures) who run the race. It is the same, Descartes suggests, with thoughts.

We are likely to agree. For all that, we might wonder whether Descartes can legitimately appeal to this principle at this stage of his argument. If he is really serious about doubting everything that can be doubted it will, one might have thought, hardly do simply to insist that this is 'highly manifest by the natural light'. After all, Hume doubted it; and perhaps the Buddha did too. So we can reasonably ask for some kind of argument here.

2. Judging *who* is in pain

We will return to this point. I want to focus now on another, connected, worry that we might raise. Suppose that Descartes *has* established that where there is a thought there must be a thinker. Will that give him everything that he needs here? There is room for doubt. Consider this remark:

> So that it must, in fine, be maintained, all things being maturely and carefully considered, that this proposition I am, I exist, is necessarily true each time it is expressed by me, or conceived in my mind. (Descartes, 1641, p. 86)

We have, for the moment, granted that whenever there is a thought there must be a thinker. But how is Descartes to move from that claim to the conclusion that the thinker who engaged in meditation yesterday is the *same* one as that which engages in meditation today? 'I' is

Descartes' label for this thinking substance. My question is: what justifies Descartes' use of the *same* label for that which thought yesterday and that which thinks today? Does not his use of the same label reflect an assumption he needs to justify?

It is tempting to dismiss this question as obviously involving some kind of confusion. After all, consider an everyday example in which someone speaks of herself. On Tuesday Mary says 'I feel rather depressed', and on Wednesday she says 'I have a sore foot'. Would it not be clearly absurd to object: we will grant that *somebody* has a sore foot today, but what justification do you have for thinking that the person who has a sore foot today is the *same* person as the one who was rather depressed yesterday – namely, the one that you call 'I'?

Yes, there would be something absurd there. But we must not let that deflect us from our challenge to Descartes. For it is crucial to remember that he is offering us a particular philosophical account of what he is. He is suggesting that the real person is something quite distinct from the human being who is 5'10" tall, has brown eyes, and so on. The real person – that to which Descartes refers when he says, for example, 'I am trying to discover what I can know' – is a non-material being that is somehow connected with this publicly observable material being. Now we cannot simply take it for granted that the assumptions that we normally make about ourselves will, or should, be acceptable to one who endorses this understanding of what each of us is.

But it might seem that when the matter is put like this the real force of Descartes' view becomes apparent. Consider Mary again. Suppose that we ask her: are you sure that it is *you* that has a red spot on your forehead? There are circumstances – admittedly rather odd ones – in which this question would be appropriate. For example, in a mirror, on the other side of a crowded room, she catches a glimpse of someone with a red spot on their forehead. Her first reaction is that it is her. But she needs to think some more, or take a closer look, to make certain. When she notices that she is the only blonde at the party, and recalls that the one with the spot had blonde hair, she is sure. Now compare that case with one in which we ask her: are you sure that it is *you* that is in pain? In this case, there would, surely, be something very odd about our question; and that is linked with the fact that there is here no question of her checking that she has 'picked out the right physical body'. Suppose that I glanced at my body to make sure, as I put it, that it is *me* that is in pain: wouldn't that reflect a serious misunderstanding of what is involved in such a case? Now Descartes, it seems, has a ready explanation of this fact. There is no question of 'checking up that

I have picked out the right body', since what has the pain is not the bodily being but, rather, the non-material mind that is the real me. Thus, I can know directly, and in a way that no one else can, that the person who has a sore foot today is the same person as the one who was rather depressed yesterday: namely, me. I can know this without doing any identifying of a particular body since what I need to identify is that the being that is in pain is a particular non-bodily entity to which I, and I alone, have immediate access.

Wittgenstein expresses the matter in this way:

> We feel then that in the cases in which 'I' is used as subject, we don't use it because we recognize a particular person by his bodily characteristics; and this creates the illusion that we use this word to refer to something bodiless, which, however, has its seat in our body. In fact *this* seems to be the real ego, the one of which it was said, 'Cogito, ergo sum'. (Wittgenstein, 1958, p. 69)

But what makes Wittgenstein so sure that this is an 'illusion'? The answer is, at least in part, this: Descartes' picture does not succeed in explaining what needs to be explained.

We *might* express what needs to be understood in this way: when I judge that 'I am in pain' I cannot be wrong in thinking that it is *me* that is in pain; and, closely linked with that, my judgement that it is me is in no way dependent on my identification of a particular set of bodily features. Now it is not completely clear why the identification of a particular *non-bodily* entity should be immune from the kinds of error that can arise when we are identifying *bodily* entities. We are, perhaps, thinking in terms of the idea that my acquaintance with this entity is so immediate that it is extraordinarily unlikely that I should misidentify it. We might reason: 'It is extraordinarily unlikely that I should mistake for blue something that is unambiguously red and is right in front of me in good lighting conditions. Well, it is like that, but more so, in the case of identifying the self.' But we need not pursue the question of how useful this particular picture is. For Wittgenstein's reply to any suggestion of this form is decisive. He remarks: 'To ask "are you sure that it's *you* who have pains?" would be *nonsensical*' (Wittgenstein, 1958, p. 67).

To see the significance of this observation we can consider an analogy. Suppose that a friend and I, who are completely lost on a pitch-black night, lose sight of each other. My friend shouts 'Where are you?', and I reply 'I'm here'. That reply is not dependent on my having identified my physical surroundings in any way; and, linked with that, it makes no sense to suppose that in saying 'I'm here' I might have got it wrong. It *makes no sense* to suppose this. The case is quite different from that in which, standing in front of an unambiguously Big Ben structure and with red double-deckers all round me, I say 'I am in London'. It would be difficult to get that wrong! But it does *make sense* to suppose that someone should get it wrong. After all, they could have – for all I know they actually have – built a replica in Disney World; and the odd forgetful visitor might get confused for a few moments. Now it is not like that with the person who, on a dark night, says 'I'm here'. In this case, as I suggested, it makes no sense to suppose that the person might have got it wrong; it makes no sense to suppose that the true answer to the question was 'I am over there'. The reason it makes no sense to suppose that one might have got it wrong is that one can correctly say 'I'm here' *even though one has no idea where one is*. The words 'I'm here' might, on the surface, look as though they are doing the same kind of work as do the words 'I'm in London'; that is to say, identifying a particular physical location as being the one where I am. But it becomes clear that they do a very different kind of work when we reflect on the fact that if I had cried out 'Help!', or simply screamed, that would have achieved precisely the same as my words do.

The situation is the same when I say 'I am in pain'. If it were like the Big Ben case it would at least make sense to suppose that I had mistaken someone else extremely like me for myself. When we acknowledge that that does not make sense we see that the matter must be approached differently. Certainly my use of the word 'I' does not rest on my identification of this particular bodily entity: this 5'10" tall, brown-eyed handsome man. But the correction that has to be made to that suggestion is, in a sense, much more radical than is suggested by the Cartesian 'immaterial mind' view. If, in saying 'I am in pain', I was identifying a particular non-bodily entity as the thing having the pain it would at least *make sense* to ask 'How do you know that it is *you* that is in pain?'. And it would at least *make sense* to suppose that I had *mis*identified the entity; for it would make sense to suppose that another very like it had taken its place. But neither the question nor the supposition make sense.

This does not, perhaps, show that the Cartesian picture of the self – that according to which the word 'I' refers to a non-material mind that has its seat in the body – is *wrong*. It does, however, undermine one of its principal attractions. For it shows, at the very least, that this picture does not have any special power to explain what we might have thought it would: namely, the peculiarities of the individual's identification of *himself* as the one who is in pain or is having a certain thought. (This argument, you may have noticed, is of exactly the same form as the 'private language argument' discussed in Chapter 4 section 3.)

3. Memory and identity

John Locke, an English philosopher who was born in 1632 and died in 1704, offers a ground-breaking discussion of the identity of a person to which all later discussions are indebted. Locke was inclined to accept the general Cartesian view of a person: he was, that is, inclined to accept that a live human being is composed of a material body linked with a non-material 'mind' or 'soul'. He was also convinced that there is a crucial distinction between what he calls, on the one hand, the 'identity of *man*', and, on the other, '*personal* identity'. He was, that is, convinced that it is one thing to say that the individual before me is the same *man* – or, as I will express it, the same *human being* – as I met last week, and quite another to say that it is the same *person* as I met last week. For he was convinced that we can envisage circumstances in which it would obviously be correct to say that a person had moved from one to another living human body:

> For should the soul of a prince, carrying with it the consciousness of the prince's past life, enter and inform the body of a cobbler, as soon as deserted by his own soul, everyone sees he would be the same *person* with the prince, accountable only for the prince's actions. (Locke, 1690, p. 216)

The force of the claim that this is the 'same person' as the prince – that this person *is* the prince – is illustrated by the last clause of the quotation from Locke: this person is 'accountable only for the prince's actions'. Despite the fact that this individual is *bodily* one and the same as the cobbler, he is to be held accountable for the prince's, not the cobbler's, past actions: thus, he is the one to be praised or blamed for the prince's good or bad actions, he is the one who is committed to keeping a promise that the prince made, and, we may suppose, he is the one to whom *I* am committed by a promise that I made to the prince. These, and other things of the same kind, are what is involved in the claim that the person in the cobbler's body is the same person as – *is* – the prince. While, then, the person before us is not *bodily* one and the same as the prince – while it is not the same 'man', the same 'human being' – it is the same 'person' as the prince.

In one sense Locke is here close to Descartes. Both hold that there is no difficulty in the idea that, for example, I should continue to exist in another body (as, perhaps, both hold that there is no difficulty in the idea that I should continue to exist in a totally disembodied form). Locke was, however, convinced that there are serious problems with the view that it is 'having the same non-material soul' that is crucial to my being the same person as one who did a certain thing in the past. The point that Locke stresses here is not so much one about my *knowledge* of who I am, but rather one about my *concern* about who I am. He argues that 'having the same non-material soul' is not something about which we can *care* in the way that we care about who we are. Locke makes his point in this way:

> Let anyone reflect upon himself, and conclude that he has in himself an immaterial spirit, which is that which thinks in him, and, in the constant change of his body keeps him the same: and is that which he calls himself; let him also suppose it to be the same soul that was in Nestor or Thersites at the siege of Troy (for souls being, as far as we know anything of them, in their nature indifferent to any parcel of matter, the supposition has no apparent absurdity in it), which it may have been, as well as it is now the soul of any other man; but he now having no consciousness of any of the actions either of Nestor or Thersites, does or can he conceive himself the same person with either of them? Can he be concerned in either of their actions? attribute them to himself, or think them his own, more than the actions of any other man that ever existed? (Locke, 1690, p. 215)

Locke takes it to be clear that the answer to these questions is 'No'. He concludes that what is crucial to the idea that a particular past thought is one that *I* had, or a particular past action one that *I* performed, is not my 'having (or "being") the same soul' as the person who had that thought or performed that action.

What *is* crucial for this is, Locke suggests, to be found by reflecting on what makes a particular thought or sensation that is *now* being undergone *my* thought or sensation. What is crucial here is, on the face of it, the fact that I am conscious – have an inside awareness – of that thought or sensation. For example, it follows from the fact that I am aware of a pain in the characteristic first personal way – that is to say, that I *feel* the pain – that the pain in question is *my* pain. Perhaps, then, we should simply extend this idea to *past* thoughts, sensations and actions: what is crucial to the idea that a particular past thought is one that *I* had, or a particular past action one that *I* performed, is the fact that I am conscious of it – have an inside awareness of it.

It follows from Locke's view that it could be true that I am the same person as the one who did a certain thing in the past even though the substance – both material and immaterial – of which I am composed is quite different. For if I have an inside memory of having done it then I *am* the one who did it; and that is so quite independently of whether this soul – the one that I 'am' or 'have' – is the one that was initially present in, for example, Nestor's or Thersites' body. If it seems odd to suggest that 'being composed of the same substance' is irrelevant to 'being the same person', we should remember, as Locke does, that we are quite ready to speak in this way in other cases. We say that this is the same tree as the one that was standing here forty years ago, even though there has been a radical change in the 'material substance' – the physical particles – of which it is composed. Some philosophers – Hume is a notable example – have been deeply suspicious of our readiness to speak in this way. But, in the absence of a decent argument, we may have to put this down to a philosophical prejudice.

Locke's view appears to do much better justice than does the 'sameness of soul' account to the idea, central to Descartes' general approach to the self, that knowledge of oneself is immediate and infallible. In the present context this is the idea that the individual herself has immediate and infallible 'inside' knowledge of who she is: for example, that she is the one who signed the documents last week. With this, Locke's view also does justice to our intuitive sense of how we should think of certain remarkable phenomena that are related to his Nestor and Thersites example. I am thinking here of the many reported cases in which a young child – characteristically one who has quite recently learned to talk – appears to have a substantial body of 'inside' knowledge of the life of a person who died before she was born. (For examples, see Stevenson, 1974.) She makes detailed claims about this person's life: claims that are substantiated by later investigation. The knowledge is 'inside' in the sense, first, that it appears that the information has not in some way been transmitted to the child by another; and, second, that she experiences the knowledge that she has of this other life as a 'memory' of it: for example, she spontaneously speaks of things that the 'remembered' person did as things that *she* has done.

Now many will, no doubt, be sceptical about the authenticity of such reports. But if such a case *could* be authenticated, many, perhaps most, might feel little hesitation in speaking of the child as the reincarnation of the earlier individual. This response, it seems, reflects our intuitive sense of the correctness of Locke's approach.

But while Locke's view has powerful attractions, it is pretty clear that, as it stands, it will not do. To see this, we must notice first that care is needed in its formulation. We might express the view in this way: 'I am the person who robbed the bank if and only if I remember robbing the bank.' Now expressions of the form 'I remember robbing the bank' are, in our normal speech, used in two rather different ways. In some cases they are used simply to report an impression that I now have. 'I distinctly remember leaving the keys on the sideboard' I say; and I continue to say 'That is how I remember it' even once it has been clearly established that I did not leave them there. But in a different use of the words 'I remember robbing the bank' or 'I remember leaving the keys on the sideboard' we will insist that if it turns out that he did not rob the bank then his words were simply not true: it *seems* to him that he remembers robbing the bank, but he doesn't really.

Now in which of these ways should we read the suggestion that *I* am the one who performed a certain action if and only if I 'remember' performing it? It seems clear that if we read it in the *second* way we lose the sense of immediate and infallible knowledge of who I am that Locke is trying to hold on to. For while it will follow from the fact that 'I remember robbing the bank' that I did rob the bank, *I* will have no special authority in judging whether I really do remember robbing the bank. Others – for example, the nurse on the psychiatric ward where I was a patient at the time of the robbery – may know better than I do that I do not *really* remember robbing the bank; it only seems to me that I remember it. Closely linked with this is the fact that, given this reading, it can hardly be said that we explain what it is for Jim to be the one who robbed the bank by saying 'He remembers doing so'; for in explaining what is required for it to be true that he really does remember we will have to speak of the fact that he is the one who robbed the bank!

Staying with this case, but switching to the *first* sense of 'remember', it can be said that I remember robbing the bank without first establishing that I *did* rob it: for to say that 'I remember robbing the bank' is simply to report an impression that I now have. In *this* sense, we might say, a person has immediate and infallible knowledge of his own memories. But taken in *this* sense, it clearly does not follow from the fact that I remember doing something that I was the one who did it. We would normally assume that it could, in practice, seem quite clear to someone that he did a certain thing and yet it not at all follow that he was the one who did it.

Further, whichever sense of 'remember' we employ here, Locke's view appears to face the following objection. There are cases in which we readily say that this is the person who did a certain thing even though she does not remember doing it. For example, there are many things that I did as a child that I do not now remember doing. Are we to say on that account that it was not really *me* who did them?

I am, in these objections, appealing to our normal views about when it can be said that this is the *same* person as one who did a certain thing in the past. I am suggesting, on these grounds, that Locke's view cannot be a satisfactory account of what we normally mean when we say this kind of thing. Now it might be replied that this only shows that our normal ways of speaking about these matters are deeply confused. It might be added that Locke is offering us a revised understanding of what is involved in our identity over time: one that is not open to the charge of 'confusion'.

Clearly that is a possible position. But the charge of 'confusion' will have to be substantiated. On the face of it, Locke has done no more than show that his view fits with at least *some* of our intuitions better than does the Cartesian alternative.

How might it be shown that one view of what is crucial to being the same person over time is to be preferred to another? Perhaps a variety of forms of argument are possible. In any case, when considering any such argument it is important to bear in mind that what is at issue here is not simply what we *say*. As Locke stresses, our views about the identity of people are closely bound up with a whole range of practices and feelings that have a central place in our lives. Locke focuses in particular on our practices of reward and punishment. We can only punish a man for a crime if *he* was the one who committed it. The same point applies to such responses to others as praise, blame, gratitude and resentment; and to feelings about oneself such as pride and guilt. Again, an understanding of *who* this is may be central to our personal relationship with another. I may feel a special commitment to this person because she is my mother: the one who gave birth to me and raised me. I may feel bound to this woman in a special way because, in a wedding ceremony, I made a commitment to stay with her until death. Perhaps more significantly, the particular character of the love or respect that I feel for another may be very closely bound up with my sense that this is a person who has, or a person with whom I share, a certain past.

It is possible that Locke did not appreciate just how deeply his account would bring him into conflict with feelings and practices that few of us will give up lightly. Rather than exploring these conflicts, however (conflicts that the reader can readily explore for herself), I will turn to a view that, while having significant affinities with Locke's, has been thought by some to avoid its most obvious difficulties.

4. 'No-self'

I mentioned earlier Hume's suggestion that when we introspect we do not find a *self* that *has* thoughts, feelings and so on; we find only the thoughts and feelings themselves. Having allowed, with characteristic irony, that there may be metaphysicians who have more luck than he does, Hume comments:

> But setting aside some metaphysicians of this kind, I may venture to affirm of the rest of mankind, that they are nothing but a bundle or collection of different perceptions, which succeed each other with an inconceivable rapidity, and are in a perpetual flux and movement. ...They are the successive perceptions only, that constitute the mind. (Hume, 1739, p. 302)

Hume's suggestion echoes ideas that are found in Buddhist thinking:

> Buddha has spoken thus: 'O Brethren, actions do exist, and also their consequences, but the person that acts does not. There is no one to cast away this set of elements and no one to assume a new set of them. There exists no Individual, it is only a conventional name, given to a set of elements.' (*Cila Mara*. Quoted: Parfit, 1984, p. 502)

Closely related ideas have a strong hold in certain quarters of contemporary Western philosophy. In particular, Derek Parfit has argued that we must understand the links between a person at different stages of her life, not in terms of some persisting individual that *has* all of the emotions, sensations and so on that we think of as hers, but in terms of certain connections between these 'mental' ('psychological') characteristics at different times. The connection, stressed by Locke, between a thought or action and a later memory of it is one such psychological link. But there are many others. There is the connection between an intention to do something and the later performance of that action. There are the connections of similarity between the beliefs, desires and interests of a person at one time and the 'same' person at a later time. More broadly, we may speak of the similarity in character between a person at one stage of his life and the 'same' person at a later stage.

Consider a human being – John Williams – who lives for 90 years, during which time he undergoes significant changes in his psychological characteristics. Between JW on any one day of his life and JW on the next day there are very close psychological connections: he has very similar beliefs and character, on the second day he remembers much of what he thought and did on the first, and so on. Such *direct* connections will be weaker over a longer time span. The beliefs and character of the 50 year old are very different from those of the 5 year old, the 50 year old has very limited memories of the 5 year old's life, and so on. Nevertheless the 50 year old is 'psychologically continuous' with the 5 year old. That is to say, his psychological characteristics developed out of those of the 5 year old through a series of stages: at each stage there being close direct psychological connections with the previous stage. In *that* sense we can say that the 50 year old is the 'same' person as the 5 year old. But once we give up the idea that the important thing is some underlying core – such as a Cartesian 'soul' – that links the 5 year old with the 50 year old we will no longer feel that this sense in which he can be said to be the 'same' person is of much significance. It is direct psychological connections that are the *significant* links between different stages of a person's life. There is a *significant,* an important, sense in which JW today is the same person as JW last year only if the person at each of these times has closely similar character, memories and so on.

Parfit's view is clearly similar to that which the Buddha seems to present. Both deny that there is some core that *underlies* the psychological elements and which is the important link between different stages of a person's life. They agree that where there has been a substantial change in psychological characteristics there is no significant, but only a 'conventional' sense in which it can be said that we have the same person. They perhaps *disagree* over what we should say where there has not been such a substantial change. While the Buddha seems to suggest that even here there is no significant sense in which it can be said that we have the same person, Parfit maintains that in such a case there *is* a significant sense in which this can be said. Closely connected with that is the fact that the Buddha is, on the face of it, calling for a much more radical revision in our current thought about ourselves than is Parfit.

One example – perhaps the central example – of the revision demanded by the Buddhist view relates to the individual's thought about his or her 'own future'. Most of us have a sense that there is a very important difference between a case in which it will be *me* who suffers pain tomorrow and a case in which someone else will suffer pain tomorrow. This sense of a deep difference is reflected in the very different feelings that we have in the two cases; and in the degree of trouble to which we are generally prepared to go to try to ensure that the pain is not felt. For the Buddha, by contrast, there is no important sense, only a conventional one, in which 'I' will be around tomorrow; a pain will be felt tomorrow, but there is no important contrast between the case in which it will, as we say, be 'me' who feels it and that in which it will be someone else. Parfit's view is less radical. There may be no important sense in which it will be 'me' who suffers some painful illness in 30 years' time; but, provided that I am closely psychologically connected with him, there is an important sense in which the person who will suffer pain tomorrow is me.

How are we to decide between the Buddha's and Parfit's interpretation of the 'no-self' view? They agree about *what* connections hold between different stages of a person's life, but disagree about the *importance* of particular connections. It might be argued that the Buddha is clearly right on the following grounds: if there is no unchanging substance at the core of our being then there is no significant sense in which I am the same person from one moment to the next. But Locke's example of the tree should remind us that we need an argument for that claim.

Parfit defends *his* point of view by appealing to what he takes to be our everyday sense of what is of value in a personal relationship. In this he follows the argument of another contemporary philosopher – Antony Quinton. Quinton writes:

> For why, after all, do we bother to identify people so carefully? What is unique about individual people that is important enough for us to call them by individual proper names? In our general relations with other human beings their bodies are for the most part intrinsically unimportant. We use them as convenient recognition devices enabling us to locate without difficulty the persisting character and memory complexes in which we are interested, which we love or like. (Quinton, 1962, p. 402)

It is quite clear, Quinton and Parfit argue, that in so far as I genuinely care for another as an individual person (as opposed, for example, to caring for her simply as a sexual object) it is her particular set of psychological characteristics that is at the centre of my understanding of her. I will, then, think of the other as, in the *important* sense, the 'same' person so long, but only so long, as she has roughly the same psychological characteristics. We should conclude that 'having the same psychological characteristics' – being 'closely psychologically connected' – is a significant – is *the* significant – connection between stages of a life. A person in 1995 is, in the *important* sense, the 'same' person as one in 1996 if and only if the one is closely psychologically connected with the other.

Parfit's and Quinton's argument appeals to certain intuitions – intuitions about what is of value in a personal relationship – that they hope their readers will share. We need not consider what a Buddhist defence of the more radical conclusion might look like – Parfit's conclusion is radical enough for us to be going on with! For while his argument appeals to intuitions that he hopes we will share, he also suggests that if we think the matter through properly we will end up with some fairly startling conclusions. For if we agree that it is 'close psychological connectedness' that is the *important* link between the different stages of a life we may find that we have to revise some of our views about, for example, punishment, long-term commitments to another, and the idea of long-term self-interest.

5. Personal identity and personal relations

The changes that might be called for here are, at least in their general outline, fairly obvious, and we need not consider them in detail. I would, however, like to consider the core of Quinton and Parfit's argument a little more carefully. The argument appeals to something that we might call our 'ethical' sense of what is of value in a personal relationship. Now there are grounds for saying that this is the *kind* of argument that is needed here. After all, our question is: which connections between the different stages of what we speak of as a 'single life' are the *important* ones? Thus, even if there *was* (as Parfit doubts that there is) an unchanging non-material core linking the different stages of a life, that would, as Locke reminds us, still leave open the question of whether this link was important in the sense that now concerns us. But do our ethical intuitions really lead us down the path that Parfit and Quinton follow?

Consider the way in which a woman might say of her husband: 'This is not the man I married'; or the way in which we might say of an elderly person who has suffered a stroke: 'She is not the person she once was.' While such expressions may seem to harmonize nicely with Parfit's view, care is needed. For it may be – indeed I think it is – that the sense of such words depends on an acceptance that there is a straightforward sense in which the person of whom we are speaking *is* the very one that we knew before. We might compare such cases with one in which I say 'This is not the car it once was'. My words, I take it, mean something like: 'It has lost many of the features it once had' – features that, perhaps, played an important role in my being initially attracted to it. But it is only true that it has 'lost' these features if, in a straightforward sense, it is the very car that once had those features; and, closely connected with that, there would, in such a case, be no possible grounds for arresting me on the basis of 'the fact that I am driving around in a car that is not mine – the one I bought ten years ago'.

While the importance that the idea of 'being the same person' has is quite different from that which the idea of 'being the same car' has, an analogue of the above point may apply there. For example, consider a case in which someone undergoes radical psychological change as the result of, say, a severe stroke. Might we not say that the particular tragedy of such cases is dependent on the idea that there is a quite straightforward sense in which this *is* the same person? It is true that children abandon their aged and decrepit parents in geriatric wards. But it is not at all clear that we should take their doing so as reflecting a doubt about who this is. Indeed, it might be in part quite the reverse. It is precisely *because* it is quite clear that this is my grandfather that the thought of visits is such a nightmare. If I did not accept so unambiguously that this is my grandfather I might be able to visit him with little discomfort; and, to mention another aspect of the same point, I might not feel the guilt that I do about not visiting him. The same point applies to the horror that a parent feels on learning that her child has suffered serious brain damage. On the view outlined by Quinton and Parfit, this would, or should, be for the parent the same as her child's death. But I take it that this suggestion involves a serious distortion of the way in which at least many people do, in practice, feel in such circumstances. There is one sense in which many might find such a situation more agonizing than one in which their child dies; for what is so dreadful about the situation is the fact that it is *John* – my child – that is in this condition.

These are extreme examples of what are, I think, familiar features of our feelings for another in the more normal cases of gradual change over time. Now it does not, of course, follow from the fact that, at least in many of us, concern for some others does take the form of which I have been speaking, that it *ought* to do so. My point is just that a little reflection may lead us to doubt whether Quinton and Parfit can really count on our intuitions at the point at which their argument needs them.

Suppose that we took as our starting point the ways in which another may continue to occupy a quite special place in our feelings despite radical changes in their characteristics. And suppose that we added to this the fact – as I think it is – that many feel that there is something particularly admirable in a 'love' in which this feature is powerful. We might add, too, the way in which my fear of a pain that 'I' will undergo tomorrow might be in no way compromised by the information that I will, before then, suffer brain damage – brain damage of a form such that the person who suffers tomorrow will be psychologically quite different from me today. Focusing on these intuitions we might be drawn to a quite different way of thinking of what is crucial to 'being the same person' over time. It seems clear that 'being the same human being' – 'being the same bodily being' – is of central importance in much of our normal thought about sameness of people. And it is not, at any rate, obvious that this is a reflection of something in our nature that we will, on reflection, wish to disown.

The tentative conclusion of this chapter is, then, that we should at least consider the possibility that Locke's enormously influential distinction between being the same 'person' and being the same 'human being' ('man') is one of which we should be suspicious.

Further reading

David Hume's discussion of personal identity can be found in *A Treatise of Human Nature*, Book I Part iv section 6. Wittgenstein's treatment of the word 'I' is to be found in *The Blue and Brown Books*, pp. 66–70. For John Locke's groundbreaking discussion see *An Essay Concerning Human Understanding*, Book II chapter 27; and for an extremely clear and detailed presentation of both the importance of Locke's contribution to the debate and the difficulties in his view see Antony Flew, 'Locke and the Problem of Personal Identity'.

Derek Parfit defends his views in his paper 'Personal Identity', and in much greater detail in his *Reasons and Persons*. Quinton's paper 'The Soul' is a more straightforward presentation of the key idea developed in Parfit's work. For a useful introduction to Buddhist views and their relation, in particular, to Parfit's position see Steven Collins' paper 'Buddhism in Recent British Philosophy and Theology'. The idea that we should not draw Locke's distinction between 'being the same person' and 'being the same man' is sometimes spoken of as the view that it is bodily continuity that is essential to personal identity. The best-known exponent of this view is Bernard Williams: see, in particular, the first four papers in his collection *Problems of the Self*. For a brief and very readable introduction to the topic of this chapter see John Perry, *A Dialogue on Personal Identity and Immortality*. See also John Perry (ed.), *Personal Identity*; this useful collection contains a number of the above papers.

9
Freedom and Science

1. Introduction

In a recent television programme on free will and punishment a central place was given to the trial of a man charged with murder. The defendant pleaded not guilty: not on the grounds that he had not killed the woman but, rather, on the grounds that he was not responsible for his actions at the time. His case turned on the claim that he had, unknowingly, been exposed to chemicals at work that had rendered him liable to extremely violent behaviour. The question at the centre of the case was then: what connection, if any, was there between the fact that he was exposed to this chemical and his violent behaviour?

The jury, in fact, decided that there was no connection and the man was convicted. Let us suppose, however, that there was strong evidence that the man would not have acted as he did if it had not been for the chemical. The presenter of the programme remarked that in these circumstances we would all agree that the man was not free and so should not be punished. I suspect that most people *would* agree. If we do, however, it might seem that we are going to have some difficulty avoiding a conclusion with which we might be rather less happy: the conclusion that none of us is ever really free in anything that we do. For it seems that we have to concede that it could be the case that everything that we do is dependent on chemicals in our brain in just this way. It could be that but for the occurrence of a particular chemical process in my brain I would not have done so well in that exam, would not have performed that generous action, and so on. Perhaps it is plausible to suppose that science will, in time, reveal that all that we do, think and feel is dependent in this kind of way on chemical processes for which the individual cannot be held responsible. (It is worth recalling here the crucial role that this assumption, or something very like it, played in the argument for physicalism discussed in Chapter 6.) At any rate, we cannot, surely, rule this possibility out. Suppose, then, that science does establish this. If we accept the reasoning that seemed plausible in the case of the man charged with murder we will, it seems, have to conclude that none of us is ever free in anything that we do. This conclusion was defended in the television programme.

2. Causes and enabling conditions

'We would all agree that, if he wouldn't have done it if it hadn't been for the chemical, he was not free.' Consider a different case. Imagine that a man on trial for murder is a diabetic and periodically requires insulin to stop him from falling into a coma. It turns out that, by pure chance, a chemical that he is sometimes exposed to at work has the same effect as the insulin. Suppose now that he murders a woman at a time when, but for the effect of the chemical, he would have been lying unconscious on the floor. That is to say, he would not have killed her had it not been for the chemical.

Is it obvious in this case that we should conclude that the man was not free? Many, I suspect, would be much more hesitant in drawing that conclusion. What, then, is the difference between this and our original case? You might be inclined to say that the difference lies in the fact that in the first case, but not the second, the chemical caused the man's violent behaviour; and that it is because of this that he is not rightly held responsible for what he did. In fact, however, I did not, in my description of the case, say that the chemical 'caused' the violent behaviour. I said only that he would not have acted as he did if it had not been for the chemical; and that much is true in the second case also. Indeed, my question 'What is the difference between the cases?' is potentially misleading. For my description of the original case was not at all detailed, and for all that I actually said the case could have been exactly the same as the second case that I described.

If, then, we do not find it obvious that the man in my second case was not free our response to the first case was too quick. In judging that the man was not free we were making an assumption that was not completely warranted by the information given. This is important in two ways. First, it shows that we need to be very careful in judging, in particular cases, that somebody is or is not rightly held responsible for his actions; we need to state very precisely just what it is that will show that an individual was not free. Second, I presented an argument that suggested that science might show that none of us is ever free in anything that we do. Now if our response to the first case was too quick then so was this argument. It does not, for example, follow immediately from the fact that I would not have performed a certain generous action if it had not been for a certain chemical process in my brain that I cannot be regarded as responsible for the action. (This should have been obvious. For after all, everything that I do is dependent in that way on the pumping of my heart; yet we do not feel that that fact shows that I am not responsible for what I do. But what should be obvious is often easily overlooked when doing philosophy.)

A crucial question here, then, is this: what is the further assumption that is needed in order to justify the conclusion that the man featured in the television programme was not free? A very natural answer to this question has already been mentioned. It might be put like this:

> What is crucial to the claim that he was not free is not simply that he would not have killed her had it not been for the chemical. What needs to be established is that the chemical *caused* him to act as he did. This was what was lacking in the second case. Certainly, in that case, the chemical played a crucial role in his acting as he did. But it did not *make* him do it. Rather, it *enabled* him to do it. Establishing in a particular case that a certain chemical caused someone to act as he did may require rather more detailed knowledge of the physiological mechanisms involved. Once that is established, however, we will certainly be able to conclude that the man was not free in acting as he did.

We might add: 'Science could establish that everything that we do is caused in a similar way, and so that we are never free.'

I believe that this very natural answer is, in a subtle way, seriously misleading. We can approach this through the question: how is it to be determined whether the chemical caused the behaviour or simply enabled the man to act in this way? What evidence would help to show which kind of case we are dealing with?

We might initially try to answer this question in this way:

> To establish that the chemical *caused* the behaviour we simply need to show that exposure to that chemical is always followed by the behaviour: that it is all that is needed for the behaviour to occur. If

it is simply that the chemical *enables* the man to act in this way then exposure to the chemical won't, by itself, be enough to produce the behaviour. Similarly, we see that putting petrol in a car does not *make* the car go when we see that putting petrol in the car isn't inevitably followed by the car going; something more is needed – namely, the turning on of the ignition.

This answer does not, as it stands, look too promising. It seems that by this test we will never be justified in saying that the chemical caused the behaviour: for it is never the case that a single condition, such as the presence of a certain chemical, is all that is needed for a certain form of behaviour to occur. Indeed, *no* causal links are such that the cause event is sufficient, in this sense, for the occurrence of the effect; there are always further background conditions that are also necessary but which, perhaps, go unstated because they can be taken for granted. In the case we are concerned with, the presence of the chemical would not lead to violent behaviour if the man was tied up, paralysed, if he had been given a dose of some inhibiting drug, and so on.

3. Freedom, science and morality

We might, at this point, be tempted to hand the question over to the scientist. It is, after all, surely the business of science to establish the causes of phenomena. We should not expect, it might be argued, that in a complex case of the kind we are now dealing with it will be possible to establish decisively the causes of a piece of behaviour without the detailed knowledge of physiology that only the scientist has. What we need is a precise understanding of the mechanism that links the breathing in of fumes from this chemical with the violent behaviour displayed by this man.

We need, I think, to take care with the questions that we hand over to the scientist. Not *all* questions are scientific questions. Further, the question 'Which questions are scientific questions?' is itself one of those that is not, or at least not exclusively, a scientific question. A consequence of this latter point is that scientists cannot always be counted on to return unanswered those questions that they have no special qualifications to answer. Now you might think that it is at least clear that questions about the causes of events are the proper business of the scientist. But while in one sense I do not want to dispute that, there is another sense in which I want to suggest that care is needed. For our question is of the form: 'Did x cause y, or did it simply enable y to happen?' And I am not at all sure that questions of *that* form are characteristically questions for the scientist.

If that suggestion seems absurd consider the following case. Jones is in hospital with two broken legs having fallen off a ladder. He and his wife are agreed that the accident would not have happened if it had been a better ladder or if he had taken more care. However, *he* says 'I'm here because she bought a cheap ladder', while *she* says 'You're here because you didn't take enough care'. An argument about this might develop in a number of different ways, and it is certainly not obvious that the scientist will have any useful contribution to make to it. For example, the wife might argue that if she had bought the more expensive ladder they would not have been able to take the kids to the pantomime and that would have been terribly unfair to them. The husband replies that kids nowadays are hopelessly spoiled. And so on. Now it seems clear that in this case the question 'What was the cause of the accident?' is not one that the natural scientist has any special qualifications to answer.

It might be replied that what, in this case, we speak of as 'trying to determine the cause of the accident' is really a matter of determining who is rightly blamed for it. The question is, in that sense, a moral one, and that is why the scientist may have little helpful to contribute to it. That is true. Indeed, it is my central point. Given a range of factors on which the occurrence of a particular event depended, the task of picking out one as 'the cause' is very often, at least in part, a moral matter. Now in the case with which I opened this chapter – that of the man charged with murder – the question 'Did the chemical cause his violent behaviour?' clearly had moral *implications:* for in deciding that, the court was deciding whether he should be punished for those acts. Further, we are assuming that it has already been established that he would not have acted as he did had it not been for the chemical. Given these points, is it clear that the specialist knowledge of the scientist is what we need in order to decide whether we should speak of the chemical as 'the cause' of the behaviour?

A consideration that was given a central place in the case featured in the television programme was this. The man had never before acted in this way, and a series of character witnesses testified that such behaviour was totally out of character. Further, there is some evidence that when others have been exposed to the chemical this has been followed by a similar tendency to violent behaviour. Now I take it that in practice most would give considerable weight to such evidence; and I do not want to suggest that we would be wrong to. What I do want to ask, however, is just *how* such evidence is supposed to support the claim that the chemical caused the violent behaviour. Suppose, for example, that we are confronted with someone who reasons in the following way:

> This evidence does nothing to show that the chemical caused the behaviour. What the chemical did was to allow this man's true self to come out for the first time. Human nature in general is fundamentally evil. A fortunate chemical imbalance in the brains of most of us stops this from coming out in our behaviour. The chemical that this man was exposed to corrected that imbalance; and so his actions were, for a brief period and for the first time, free.

No doubt we will ask what grounds this individual has for viewing the matter in this way. I introduce him, however, simply in order to focus attention on the question: what grounds do *we* have for viewing the case in the way that we are inclined to?

'But the man who argues in that way is a lunatic! And a pretty nasty one at that. You cannot be asking us to accept that he poses a serious threat to our normal view of the matter: that we should be seriously rethinking our normal view in the light of this other way of looking at the case.' No. But I am asking you to accept that a consideration of this 'lunatic', and our response to him, casts serious doubt on the suggestion that our questions here are ones that it is the business of science to resolve. It casts doubt on that suggestion precisely because it is clear that this man's argument should not be taken seriously. For if the fundamental question here was one that called for the specialist knowledge of the scientist it *could* turn out that this 'lunatic' was in fact correct.

I have been considering the suggestion that we can establish that this man was not responsible for his actions, and so is not to be blamed or punished for them, by establishing that the chemical caused his violent behaviour. I said that this suggestion involves a subtle confusion. The confusion is this. Certainly there is a close link between the judgement that the chemical caused the behaviour and the claim that we should not judge the man in the light of this behaviour: he is to be treated, not punished. We are, however, inclined to think that our view of how we should think about and treat the man is grounded in our judgement as to whether the chemical did or did not cause his behaviour. I am suggesting that it might be closer to the truth to say that it is the other way round; or, perhaps better, that we have here two formulations of a single question. In saying that the chemical 'caused' the behaviour we are not giving a neutral report of a scientific finding from which we can draw conclusions about how he is to be thought of and treated. The judgement that the case is to be described in that way is, rather, in itself an expression of our view of how we should think of and treat the man. In the case of the husband and wife arguing about the accident, the question 'What was the cause of the accident?' pretty well just *is* the question 'Where does the moral fault lie?'; that is, what is needed to resolve the first question (if it is to be resolved) may be more akin to moral than to scientific reasoning. Similarly, the question 'Did the chemical cause the behaviour or did it simply enable the man's true self to come out?' may pretty well just *be* the question 'Is the man to be blamed and punished for what he did?'; that is, again, what is needed to resolve the first question may be more akin to moral than to scientific reasoning.

Now the importance of this is, in part, that it shows that there is no straightforward move from a consideration of this kind of case to the conclusion that none of us is ever free in anything that we do. I do not, in saying this, mean to rule out the possibility of an argument that might move us in this general direction. Perhaps it could be shown that the area in which we should think of ourselves as fully responsible is much more limited than we now suppose; or, more dramatically, that our current understanding of the way in which people should sometimes be held responsible for what they do should be radically modified. But my point is, rather, a point about the kind of argument that would be needed to establish claims of this form. We are tempted to think that scientific investigation could reveal that all human behaviour is caused in a way that is incompatible with the idea that it is free. Now it is true that science has shown us, and will continue to show us, that our behaviour is dependent on a range of physiological conditions for which we are not responsible and of which we are largely ignorant. In showing us this, science is showing us ways of controlling human behaviour that bypass the *person* – the *human being* – altogether: it does this, for example, in its discovery of mood-controlling drugs. Science, that is, may make it easier for us to think of human behaviour, or some of it, as simply a natural phenomenon to be predicted and controlled as best we can; it may, in that way, make it easier for us to give up the idea that human beings should be held responsible for what they do – 'held responsible', that is, in a way any different from that in which a tree is held responsible for the swaying of its branches in the wind. But in showing us the detailed dependence of a certain form of behaviour on a certain physiological condition science is not showing us that that physiological condition is 'the cause' of the behaviour. For the distinction between a 'cause' and an 'enabling condition' is not, or not exclusively, a scientific one. To claim that the physiological condition is 'the cause' of the behaviour is to make a claim about how that condition should feature in our thought about that behaviour. And science cannot show us that we ought to change our thinking in this way. It cannot, for example, show us that our response to good or ill treatment should be, not gratitude or resentment, but rather a search for ways of controlling such behaviour in the future. (You might find it helpful in this connection to look again at the example of the meteor that didn't fall on Edinburgh, which I employed in my examination of the argument for materialism: see Chapter 5 section 4. That no gigantic meteor fell on Edinburgh in 1948 was a necessary condition of my birth; but it is far from clear that it follows immediately from that that it should be spoken of as one of the causes of my birth.)

In practice, we are, I take it, thinking of larger and larger areas of our lives in roughly those terms. We are, for example, much more ready to accept that certain forms of antisocial behaviour reflect a condition that is to be *treated*, as opposed to inherent wickedness that is to be punished. With this, few will be tempted to say, in the case with which I opened this chapter, that we should think of the chemical as correcting a physiological imbalance in the brain of those exposed to it, so allowing their fundamentally evil nature to find expression. I have very little hesitation in saying that this development in our thinking is, for the most part, to be welcomed. But the gains here may be closely linked with possible changes in our thinking that many would regard as grievous losses. A world without blame or punishment may well have its attractions. But what of a world in which another's act of kindness is on the same level as any natural event that benefits me: a world, that is, in which the expression of kindness brings no pleasure in itself? Or what of a world in which my grief on the death of a loved one is thought of as a physiological condition to be treated with drugs? Well, people will no doubt, even after careful reflection, have different views about the ideal we should aspire to here; and this chapter has made no contribution to that question. My aim has simply been to cast doubt on a familiar picture of the kind of reasoning needed in order to determine how we ought to be thinking in this area: a familiar picture of the role that science should play in our understanding of people and their actions. And 'cast doubt' is the very most I can hope to have done. For my target has been only one of a number of ways in which it might be thought that science poses a threat to our understanding of our actions as free. I hope, however, that what I have said is enough to indicate one possible area of doubt about whether, as I expressed the matter in Chapter 6, the language of physicalism is helpful and illuminating. To express what is basically the same point in another way: in its confident assumption that all of those physiological conditions on which my behaviour is dependent are *causes* – or may be shown by science to be causes – of my behaviour (as opposed to enabling conditions), the argument for physicalism may be begging crucial *ethical* questions about our relations with other human beings.

4. 'Could have done otherwise'

It might be thought that scientific discoveries concerning the physiological mechanisms underlying our behaviour could create a problem for our normal ideas of responsibility in a way that bypasses the distinction between 'causes' and 'enabling conditions'. For could science not reveal that the various forces acting on and within our bodies make our behaviour necessary in this sense: none of us could ever act other than we do? And is it not clear that the fact that a person could not have done other than he did is sufficient to undermine any claim that he is responsible for his action?

Well, there are a number of ways in which philosophers have argued that that is *not* so clear. We can focus on just one of these, as it is presented in an article by Harry G. Frankfurt:

> Suppose someone – Black, let us say – wants Jones to perform a certain action. Black is prepared to go to considerable lengths to get his way, but he prefers to avoid showing his hand unnecessarily. So he waits until Jones is about to make up his mind what to do, and he does nothing unless it is clear to him (Black is an excellent judge of such things) that Jones is going to decide to do something *other* than what he wants him to do. If it does become clear that Jones is going to decide to do something else, Black takes effective steps [perhaps manipulating the minute processes of Jones's brain and nervous system] to ensure that Jones decides to do, and that he does do, what he wants him to do … Now suppose that Black never has to show his hand because Jones, for reasons of his own, decides to perform and does perform the very action Black wants him to perform. (Frankfurt, 1969, pp. 835–6)

In these circumstances Jones could not have acted other than he did. And yet it seems clear that that fact casts no doubt on the idea that he is responsible for what he did. For, as things in fact turned out, the presence of Black did not, in practice, make any difference at all to what happened. Jones did what he did for his own reasons, and just as he would have done had Black not existed at all.

If these points are correct, the fact that a person could not have done other than he did is *not* sufficient to undermine the claim that he is responsible for his action. And so the argument of the first paragraph of this section does not go through. Even if science did establish that none of us could ever do other than what we do it would not follow that none of us is ever responsible for anything that we do. Frankfurt's example also, perhaps, provides a clue as to where we should be looking for one of the keys to the idea of 'responsibility'. What makes it clear to us that, despite the fact that Jones could not have acted other than he did, he is still responsible for his action is that he performs the action *for his own reasons*. To show us that none of us is ever responsible for anything that we do the scientists would have to show us that none of us ever acts as we do for the reasons that we offer in explanation or justification of our actions.

I will not address directly the question of whether science might show us *that*. Instead, I want to mention another way in which we may have a misleading picture of the character of the threat that scientific advances might pose to our normal ideas of responsibility.

5. Responsibility and the person

When we start to think about the internal – physiological – causes of human behaviour ('behaviour'?) we can easily find ourselves caught within a narrow range of – rather unattractive – options. For it can seem obvious to us that it is these physiological mechanisms that are *really* responsible for the behaviour. There seems to be no place here for the *person*: no place for the idea that the *person* makes some contribution to what happens. It may then seem that the only way to create a place for the person would be to think in traditional dualist terms: to think, that is, in terms of the real person being a 'mind' or 'soul', that acts *on* a particular point of the physiological system from a position *outside* that system. And if we have doubts about that escape route, we may find ourselves confronted with a paradox. For we started off with the idea that what creates a problem for our thought of our actions as free is *determinism* – the idea that all physical happenings are the necessary product of prior causal conditions. But now suppose that (as apparently the scientists tell us) some of what happens in the micro-world that they study is *in*deterministic. And suppose that at some point in the chain of events leading up to the rising of ('my raising'?) my arm there is an event that is not a necessary upshot of any prior conditions. My behaviour, let us suppose, is the result, in part, of a random swerve of a sub-atomic particle. Would that in any way help the idea that I am in some sense responsible for what 'I did'? If not, then the situation is much worse than we originally thought: for there is, it seems, no place in the world for freedom *whether or not* everything that happens is deterministically dictated.

Perhaps, however, this fact – the fact that determinism seems, in this sense, to be irrelevant to the question of freedom – should alert us to the possibility that something has gone wrong at some point in our thinking. In one formulation, I suggested that when we reflect on the internal causes of behaviour our idea of responsibility seems to face difficulties because there seems to be no place here for the *person*. The Cartesian approach attempts to locate a place for the person from within the arena of internal causes. It suggests that at some point within the neurophysiological sequence of causes and effects we will find a gap: this being the point at which the person injects her contribution to what happens. Now I have suggested in previous chapters that this is not the place to look for the person. The person is the human being. It is, then, no wonder that when our attention is focused on the internal causes of behaviour we can find no place for the idea that the person makes some contribution to what happens. For the *person* is not to be found at this level – any more than the beauty of the painting, or the smile on the lips of the woman portrayed, is to be found at the level revealed to us when we study the canvas through a microscope.

The idea that we find what is *really* going on, or what something *really* is, by considering the micro-world revealed to us by the physicist is one that runs deep. There are, no doubt, readings of that idea such that there is truth in it. But it is an idea that can lead us badly astray – as it does when we search in vain within the micro-world for the person.

One of the philosophical concerns that arises when we reflect on the problem of freedom and determinism is, I have suggested, not so much to do with determinism – with the idea that everything that happens happens of necessity – as with what is, in a sense, a stage prior to this. It is a concern about the idea of the individual of whom we may ask: 'Is she to be held responsible – is she to be praised, blamed, or whatever – for what happened?' In the absence of an individual about whom this question may arise, there is simply no place for philosophical worries about freedom, or responsibility.

To identify the individual as the human being is not to resolve the philosophical worries about freedom, or responsibility. But it does, perhaps, make a significant contribution to setting those concerns in their proper context. For it may draw our attention back to the ways in which, in our relations with other human beings, questions about whether an individual is to be held responsible for her actions arise, and are discussed, in practice. In Chapter 7, I followed Wittgenstein in connecting the idea that the person – the being who, for example, feels pain – is the human being with ways in which it is to the *human being* that, for example, we respond with pity: 'one does not comfort the hand, but the sufferer: one looks into his face'. And I suggested that it might be a mistake to suppose that we must seek a justification – such as that attempted by the argument from analogy – for taking the beings that I see around me to be of a kind such that it is appropriate for me to feel pity towards them in certain circumstances. Similarly, the idea that the being who acts is the human being should be taken with the fact that it is to the *human being* that we respond with resentment, gratitude, moral praise or blame, and so on, on account of what he has done: we thank, and smile at, the human being (not the hand that held the gift); we punish the human being; we reason with the human being, trying to persuade her to act differently in future; and so on. With that, it might be argued, it is a mistake to suppose that I must seek a justification – for example, by finding gaps in the physiological story – for responding, in certain circumstances, to the beings that I see around me with resentment, gratitude and so on. That is not to say that it is impossible to criticize particular responses of resentment or gratitude, or to argue for more or less radical changes in our current practices. It is, however, to say something about the forms that such criticism or argument might take.

One range of examples of what I have in mind here relates to the discussion of the previous section. For example, there are ways in which we may see – perhaps through talking with her and observing her behaviour in a wide range of circumstances – that the reasons that a particular individual offers for her actions are not, in fact, what are doing the real work in leading her to act as she does. Again, we may come to think that a person's brutalizing upbringing makes it quite unreasonable to expect him to be moved by the kinds of consideration that move most of us. It is, in part, in ways such as these that we come to judge that an individual is not fully responsible for his or her actions. And such judgements are, one might think, likely to be grounded primarily in a study of the human being's *life*, rather than in a study of her physiology.

Further reading

The literature on this topic is vast. Two recent, readable, introductory books are Susan Wolf, *Freedom Within Reason*, and Ted Honderich, *How Free Are You?*. For an excellent collection of papers on the topic see Gary Watson (ed.), *Free Will*; the introduction to this volume gives a useful overview of the philosophical treatment of this issue. The reading listed below focuses on literature that has particular relevance to the approach that I have followed in this chapter.

One of the most influential papers on this topic over the last forty years is Peter Strawson, 'Freedom and Resentment'; Strawson defends the idea, which has close analogies with Wittgenstein's thinking, that to attain a proper view of these issues we must take as our starting point the ways in which we do, in practice, care about the actions of others. Strawson is, in part, criticizing the idea that the practices of punishment, moral condemnation, and so on are to be justified in terms of their efficacy in regulating behaviour in socially desirable ways: an idea that is defended in P.H. Nowell-Smith, 'Freewill and Moral Responsibility'. Strawson's ideas are subjected to sympathetic criticism in Gary Watson, 'Responsibility and the Limits of Evil: Variations on a Strawsonian Theme'; Watson brings out vividly some of the deep tensions in our normal thinking about these matters.

The 'could have done otherwise' argument of section 4 comes from Harry G. Frankfurt, 'Alternate Possibilities and Moral Responsibility'. Another important paper by the same author, which introduces considerations of a kind on which I have not touched, is Harry G. Frankfurt, 'Freedom of the Will and the Concept of a Person'.

The notion of acting for *reasons* is given a central place in A.C. MacIntyre, 'Determinism'. A clear overview of an important thread in the discussion of these issues, in which both Strawson's and MacIntyre's papers are discussed, can be found in Daniel C. Dennett, 'Mechanism and Responsibility'. Dennett's *Elbow Room* is also provocative and suggestive.

A fuller development of some of the ideas in this chapter can be found in Lars Hertzberg, 'Blame and Causality'.

10
Postscript: The Self and the World

1. Souls, brains and human beings

According to traditional dualism, of the kind defended by Descartes, a live human being is a compound of two, intimately conjoined, parts: a material body, which is an object in the world along side other material things, and a non-material mind, which is an essentially thinking thing. The real me – 'the self' – is the second; and that is to say, the real me does not have a *life* in the normal sense. The real me does not move the furniture, dig the garden, comfort my friend who is sad or depressed, hug my wife, hide from another's anger, shout at or hit out at the one who has hurt me, and so on. Since all of these activities involve the body, and since that is not strictly part of *me*, it is not strictly me that does these things. All that *I*, strictly speaking, do is think – in Descartes' broad sense of that term in which it includes understanding, willing, imagining, perceiving and so on. Some of my thoughts cause this body – my body – to move in certain ways: as when, as we colloquially put it, 'I' dig the garden.

There are a range of possible variations on, or alternatives to, this traditional dualist picture. An alternative that is sometimes thought of as being diametrically opposed to it involves the claim that the real me – that is, the mind: the part that thinks – is not, as Descartes argues, a non-material thing. The mind is, itself, just another material entity: namely, the brain. This view, or something like it, is what many have in mind when they speak of 'materialist' views of the self.

A central claim of this book has been that what the above two views *share* is, at least from one point of view, very much more important than what they differ over. For these views share a distinctively philosophical conception of 'the mind'. They agree in the claim that the real me – the 'mind': the part that thinks, feels and so on – is something distinct from the bodily being that (brain surgeons aside!) others see or touch. They differ only in their views about the nature of this entity. The alternative that has been presented in this book involves the idea that the real me – the thing that thinks, feels, and so on – is the *human being*: one and the same being as that which moves the furniture, comforts my friends, and so on. In rejecting the idea that I am somehow 'lodged in' this body, we are not rejecting the idea that people have minds. We are simply rejecting a certain philosophical picture of what it is to 'have a mind'. To take a rough analogy, one can deny that the shape of a vase is *part* of the vase, or a distinct entity that exists along side the vase in some other realm, without denying that vases have shapes. Now, much as in speaking of the shape of a vase we are speaking of a certain aspect of the vase itself, so in speaking of a person's mind we are speaking of a certain aspect of the human being. A vase's, or for that matter a person's, physical qualities – size, shape, weight and so on – are not qualities of one *part* of the vase, or person. And no more are a person's mental qualities and activities – intelligence, sense of humour, thoughts and so on – qualities and activities of one *part* of him. A person's physical qualities and activities, on the one hand, and his mental qualities and activities, on the other, are both qualities and activities of a single thing: the human being.

I spoke of the picture of 'the mind' that has been rejected in this book as a *philosophical* picture. It is a philosophical picture in the sense that it is a picture that many find tempting when they start to think philosophically about what a person is. But it is philosophical too in the sense that it is a picture that has a powerful hold on our understanding of the activity of philosophy itself. At one level this is seen in the idea that philosophy is essentially an activity of *part* of us: an activity of 'the thinking bit'. Thus we may think that when we come into the seminar room we leave behind us all the mess of our everyday, bodily, life: that we can, and must, engage in the discussion as a purely thinking being. I suspect that this aspect of our understanding of ourselves as philosophers is seen in the massive split that we sometimes allow between what we say in the seminar room and how we live our lives in practice. In the seminar room we will say 'Morality is simply a matter of personal preference' or 'You can never really know what another is feeling or thinking', when it is clear that we do not, in practice, seriously accept these claims in our lives: for example, back on the street so to speak, we respond without hesitation to the groaning man with the dreadful wound, and would look aghast at the passer-by who, casually glancing at the injured man, said 'You can never really know what another is feeling', and walked on.

In this final chapter I want to consider another, rather different, way in which our philosophical thinking may be strongly conditioned by the kind of mind–body dualism that has been rejected in this book.

2. Descartes and 'the external world'

In Chapter 1 we looked at the relation between Descartes' conception of what he is and his suggestion that knowledge of the world of material things is dependent on knowledge of God. On the basis of his doubt about the existence of the material world Descartes builds an argument for the claim that he is something quite distinct from any material being. Thus, Descartes concludes that he lies outside the world of material things, and so his knowledge of that world is dependent on certain 'effects' that it has on him. When he 'sees and feels' a chair what he is immediately aware of is not the material object itself but simply a state of himself that he assumes is caused by the chair. And so it is only through a demonstration of the existence of a truthful and benevolent God that he can have any grounds for believing that there *is* a material world at all, or that that world is at all as he normally takes it to be.

It is, however, possible that there is a relation between Descartes' doubt and his conception of what he is that runs in, so to speak, the opposite direction.

In the Preface to the *Meditations* Descartes offers the following advice to potential readers: 'I would advise none to read this work, unless such as are able and willing to meditate with me in earnest, to detach their minds from commerce with the senses, and likewise to deliver themselves from all prejudice' (Descartes, 1641, p. 73). He adds, in the Synopsis, that the utility of the doubt on which he is about to embark lies, in part, in the fact that: 'it delivers us from all prejudice, and affords the easiest pathway by which the mind may withdraw itself from the senses' (Descartes, 1641, p. 75). We should, I think, be struck by the way in which Descartes speaks in the same breath of 'delivering us from prejudice' and 'detaching ourselves from the senses'. It is true that he later offers what he suggests are reasons for being suspicious of the senses. But my point at the moment is that, even before he asks himself what it is possible to doubt, he takes it to be clear that detachment from the senses is a goal to which we must aspire if we are to embark on a serious search for truth. Indeed, he offers the fact that it will help us to achieve this detachment as a reason for following the path of doubt. Now this is rather startling in that we might have supposed that any serious search for truth will necessarily make extensive use of the senses. Is not the person who closes her eyes and blocks her ears precisely the one who does *not* want to know the truth?

Well, there are, no doubt, certain areas in which the search for truth might be aided by closing one's eyes and blocking one's ears. Mathematics might be one. And so perhaps philosophy is another. (For many, after all, the idea of philosophy is indissolubly associated with armchairs!) But to think that Descartes' starting point might be defended in this way is to misunderstand the character of his enterprise. For Descartes' aim is not to establish whether there is one particular class of truths that can be known: philosophical truths. He is concerned to establish whether *anything* can be known. And yet he insists, apparently without argument, that one of the most familiar grounds for a claim to know something – namely, the fact that I observed what I claim to know – is not to be taken seriously.

Is it possible that assumptions about what he himself is – or, at any rate, assumptions about his relation to the material world that surrounds him – are at work at the very start of Descartes' thinking? Is he assuming that the contact between my hand and the table is not quite the unmediated contact between *me* and the table that we might have supposed; and so that the knowledge of the table that I take myself to have through the sense of touch is not quite what it seems? This suspicion is, perhaps, reinforced when we remember the ease with which Descartes moves between supposing, on the one hand, that 'the sky, the air, the earth' and so on do not exist and, and on the other, that he himself is 'without hands, eyes, flesh, blood, or any of the senses'. He seems, from the start, to be thinking of his own body as simply one object among the others he encounters in the world. As we might put it, he seems to be thinking of his own hands, eyes, and so on as things that he *comes across* in the world, rather than as being part of himself: the self that comes across things in the world, believes that that is a bull in the field, doubts whether the floor will support his weight, and so on. With that, he finds no difficulty in the idea that it might make sense to ascribe beliefs and doubts to a being – namely, himself – who, 'lacking a body', lacks a life in which there is a place for avoiding that field, or treading gingerly on the floor boards.

Perhaps, then, Descartes' idea that one who is seriously engaged in the pursuit of truth must doubt the existence of the material world *depends on* a picture of what he himself is. For if I were a bodily being – a being in the same world as that of trees and tables – then there would, it seems, be no room for a doubt about the existence of that world. So if Descartes is to drive a wedge – a place for his doubt – between 'me' and 'the world', then my body must lie on the side of *the world*.

Modern versions of Descartes' story do not speak of 'non-material minds' and 'evil demons'. They speak instead of the possibility that I might be a brain in a vat being manipulated by a mad scientist. But if you have felt some sympathy for the general direction of argument of this book you will not be inclined to think that the difference between disembodied souls, on the one hand, and brains in vats, on the other, is of great importance. What separates the idea that the 'real me' is an immaterial mind from the idea that it is a material brain is of far less significance than what separates both of those from the idea that I am the *human being*: the being that others encounter in their relations with me. For if one holds the latter view one is, as I have said, going to have difficulty identifying the point at which the demon, or mad scientist, works his evil deed. If I am this human being, and if, with that, there is no room for doubt about whether this human being exists, can there really be room for doubt about the existence of other solid bodies with which I, this human being, am in constant interaction? The point here, it should be stressed, is not simply that I am in *causal* interaction with the world: that the world has effects on me and I have effects on the world. Both the dualist and the mind–brain identity theorist can acknowledge that. We might, rather, express the point in this way: if there is no room for doubt about the existence of this embodied being – me – there is no room for a doubt that the movements of this being are sometimes impeded by other extended, tangible, beings.

3. Knowledge and action

But perhaps the matter is better expressed in terms of a certain picture of knowledge. As a recent author has expressed the view that we find in Descartes: 'To know reality is to have a correct representation of things – a correct picture within of outer reality' (Taylor, 1989, p. 144). It is of no consequence whether we think of this representation as being an image in an immaterial mind or as being a neural structure in a brain. For both approaches are equally marked off from one that understands knowledge, not in terms of the notion of *picturing*, but in terms of that of *acting*. The Cartesian paradigm of one who knows the way through the wood is a mind or brain with a 'representation' of the path; and the Cartesian paradigm of one who knows that a stone is approaching his head, or that he is confronted with another in pain, is a mind or brain with the appropriate 'representation'. The alternative paradigm will speak instead of a human being walking confidently through the wood, a human being ducking, a human being responding with pity and help, and so on. It is in seeing someone behave in these ways that we see most clearly and directly someone who has knowledge of the situation with which she is confronted.

I spoke of these as alternative 'paradigms' of knowledge. It is, of course, clear that one may know or believe something yet not act in the ways in question. The point can be put by saying that these cases are secondary. If we maintain that, despite the fact that he does nothing about it, Jones knows or believes that his daughter is in severe pain then some special explanation is needed. On the Cartesian view, it is the reverse. Knowledge or belief is, in itself, simply an inner mirroring of outer reality. It is when my knowledge finds expression in action that we need to postulate some further factor that explains its doing so.

But isn't it the Cartesian who is right here? It is being suggested that we see someone who knows that a stone is approaching her head, or someone who knows that she is confronted with a person in pain, in seeing someone who ducks out of the stone's path, or who responds to the other with help and sympathy. But, it will be said, this cannot be right since one who, for example, knows that a stone is flying towards her head will only duck if she also *desires* not to be hit by the stone. We must, then, think of the behaviour that we see, not as in some sense *being* knowledge, but as being the *product* of a certain combination of knowledge and desire. The knowledge itself must be an inner state that, in conjunction with certain desires or feelings, has certain behaviour as a causal upshot.

The idea that all human behaviour is to be explained in terms of a combination of beliefs and desires that cause it is one that has a very powerful hold within philosophical thinking about a wide range of issues. Yet it is not, it should be noted, an idea that seems to be reflected in our normal ways of thinking and speaking of human behaviour. We ask 'Why is he calling the doctor?' and receive the reply 'Because his daughter has broken her leg'. We ask 'Why did she duck?' and receive the reply 'Because the stone was heading straight for her'. The replies, which make no reference to desires, explain her behaviour by pointing to her reasons for acting in these ways: that is to say, features of her situation – not of herself – that she might offer in justification of what she did.

Now to this it is commonly replied that we only take these to be adequate explanations because we take it for granted that the individual has the desire to help his daughter, or the desire not to be hit by a stone; we can, in cases like these, safely omit reference to the desire in question because such desires are sufficiently widespread not to require explicit mention. Well, perhaps. But in the absence of some kind of argument for this claim we might wonder whether it is not just the product of the philosophical picture of knowledge that we are calling into question. If we think of knowledge or belief as being an 'inner' representation of an 'outer' reality then we will think that something else is needed – a desire – if knowledge is to be converted into action. But if we don't picture the matter in that way we may be more ready to take our normal ways of speaking at face value.

Despite the Cartesian emphasis on the individual's own immediate access to his or her own mental states, the pictures philosophers offer of our 'inner life' often seem to bear little close scrutiny. Does introspection reveal that when I duck to avoid an approaching stone, or stop to help someone in pain, my behaviour is preceded by an inner combination of belief and desire? Isn't the Cartesian simply 'finding' whatever he has decided that his theory needs? Now we should not, perhaps, make too much of this kind of objection; for the Cartesian image of infallible self-knowledge is not one that we should accept. Still, if we take as our *starting point*, not the isolated observer of the passing scene, but the human being responding to the world in which she is placed, we may arrive at a very different picture of the individual's knowledge of the world.

4. An 'absolute conception'

Wittgenstein writes:

> Language – I want to say – is a refinement, *im Anfang war die Tat* ('in the beginning was the deed') (Wittgenstein, 1976, p. 420)

> ... it is a primitive reaction to tend, to treat, the part that hurts when someone else is in pain ... (Wittgenstein, 1967, §540)

> I want to regard man here as an animal; as a primitive being to which one grants instinct but not ratiocination. As a creature in a primitive state. Any logic good enough for a primitive means of communication needs no apology from us. Language did not emerge from some kind of ratiocination. (Wittgenstein, 1969, §475)

Pity, one may say, is a form of conviction that someone else is in pain. (Wittgenstein, 1968, §287)

It is in a similar spirit that Heidegger writes:

[T]he less we just stare at the hammar-Thing, and the more we seize hold of it and use it, the more primordial does our relationship to it become, and the more unveiledly is it encountered as that which it is – as equipment. (Heidegger, 1962, p. 98)

Our discussion, in Chapter 7, of Wittgenstein's remark 'My attitude towards him is an attitude towards a soul' drew on ideas that are closely linked with these passages. I suggested that we must consider the possibility that the special range of attitudes that I have towards other human beings does not require the underpinning of some *belief* that I hold about them: the possibility that the attitudes are what is most basic in my relation to another. Now we briefly considered an objection to this proposal – an objection that might be more fully articulated in this way:

To take such reactions as *given* is to acquiesce in a picture of the world that is thoroughly coloured by our own reactions to what we encounter. Is it not central to the task of the philosopher that she stands back from her natural reactions to her experience and asks whether these reactions are really justified in view of that with which she is confronted? Is it not central to the task of the philosopher that she tries to articulate what might be called an 'absolute conception' of the world: a picture of the world that would be accessible to, and acceptable to, any rational being no matter how that being may differ from us in its natural reactions to the world? For example, while I may pull away in disgust from slugs or spiders I must recognize that this is simply a reflection of a personal peculiarity, and so should not take my reaction to embody a recognition of 'the objective disgustingness of slugs and spiders'. My ambition should be to form a picture of the world that is not, in that sense, coloured by my own responses to what I encounter.

This has been a central ambition of many philosophers. It is an ambition that is reflected in images of the person as, first and foremost, a mind that passively receives impressions from the world. The Cartesian picture of the self as a being that is radically distinct from the bodily being – the being in the world with its rich set of responses to what it encounters – may have its deepest roots here: in an image of real knowledge as involving a pure mirroring of a situation.

That ideal is one that has a powerful hold on many – perhaps most – who are drawn to philosophy. It may constitute a formidable obstacle to a full acceptance of the image of a person that has been defended in this book. The other side of this, of course, is that a proper assimilation of this image may weaken the hold of that ideal. That is not to say that we will give up the idea that we have an obligation to try to think straight: an obligation to overcome the blindness, prejudice and so on that often clouds our understanding of a situation that confronts us. It *is* to say that we will look for other models of what might be involved in doing that. The Cartesian model of clear thinking – that which involves disengagement from my responses to what confronts me – is not the only possible model. To see this, one should broaden the range of one's examples. For example, might I not feel that it is when I see a film of people caught up in war or famine that I appreciate for the first time what is really happening there? The case that I want to focus on here is not one in which I 'learn new facts' about what is going on, but rather one in which my feelings become engaged in a way in which they were not before. In such a case, it is not, we might feel, that my engagement involves colouring, but rather that my previous *dis*engagement involved blindness.

That is a controversial example. And the above quotations from Wittgenstein and Heidegger are not only controversial, but difficult too. Closely linked with that, the Cartesian picture of knowledge, and the associated conception of the task of philosophy, are extraordinarily resilient. I do not for one second suppose that what I have said in this chapter might be sufficient to break the hold of those ideas. My aim has simply been to give some indication of how questions about the nature of a person that have been central to this book might be linked with questions about knowledge that have always been central to philosophy.

Further reading

The different paradigms of knowledge, and their relation to particular views of the self, are discussed in Charles Taylor, *Sources of the Self*: see especially chapter 8, on Descartes, and chapter 9, on Locke. In *Descartes: the Project of Pure Enquiry*, Bernard Williams develops the notion of an 'absolute conception' of the world, and discusses the importance such a notion has in Descartes' thinking. Two clear and accessible books that help to place Wittgenstein's thought in relation to the issues raised in this chapter are Fergus Kerr, *Theology After Wittgenstein*, and Oswald Hanfling, *Wittgenstein's Later Philosophy* (see especially chapter 7). A useful introduction to Heidegger's thought is Stephen Mulhall, *Heidegger and Being and Time*; chapter 1 is of most relevance to the concerns of this chapter.

Bibliography

Armstrong, D.M. and Malcolm, Norman, *Consciousness and Causality* (Oxford: Blackwell, 1984).

Badham, Paul and Badham, Linda, *Immortality or Extinction?* (London: Macmillan Press – now Palgrave, 1982).

Churchland, P.M., 'Eliminative Materialism and the Propositional Attitudes', *Journal of Philosophy*, 78 (1981) 67–90.

Churchland, P.M., *Matter and Consciousness* (Cambridge, Mass.: MIT Press, 1984).

Cockburn, David, 'The Mind, the Brain and the Face', *Philosophy*, 60 (1985) 477–93.

Cockburn, David, 'Human Beings and Giant Squids', *Philosophy*, 69 (1994) 135–50.

Cockburn, David, *Other Human Beings* (Basingstoke: Macmillan Press – now Palgrave, 1990).

Collins, Steven, 'Buddhism in Recent British Philosophy and Theology', *Religious Studies*, 21 (1985) 475–93.

Cook, John, 'Human Beings', in Peter Winch (ed.) *Studies in the Philosophy of Wittgenstein* (London: Routledge & Kegan Paul, 1969).

Cottingham, John, *Descartes* (London: Phoenix, 1997).

Crane, Tim, 'Reply to Pettit', *Analysis*, 53 (4) (1994) 224–7.

Crane, Tim, *The Mechanical Mind* (Harmondsworth: Penguin, 1995).

Crane, Tim and Mellor, D.H., 'There is No Question of Physicalism', *Mind*, 99 (1990) 185–206.

Davidson, Donald, 'Mental Events', in Davidson, *Essays on Actions and Events* (Oxford University Press, 1980).

Davidson, Donald, 'Actions, Reasons and Causes', in Davidson, *Essays on Actions and Events* (Oxford University Press, 1980).

Davidson, Donald, 'Agency', in Davidson, *Essays on Actions and Events* (Oxford University Press, 1980).

Dennett, Daniel C., 'Mechanism and Responsibility', in Dennett, *Brainstorms* (Montgomery, Vermont: Bradford Books, 1978).

Dennett, Daniel C., *Elbow Room* (Oxford University Press, 1984).

Descartes, René, *Meditations on the First Philosophy* (1641), *Discourse on Method* (1637), *Principles of Philosophy* (1644), all in Descartes, *A Discourse on Method*, trans. John Veitch, (London: Dent, 1962).

Diamond, Cora, 'Eating Meat and Eating People', in Diamond, *The Realistic Spirit* (Cambridge, Mass.: MIT Press, 1991).

Dilman, Ilham, *Love and Human Separateness* (Oxford: Blackwell, 1987).

Dreyfus, Hubert L., *What Computers Still Can't Do* (Cambridge, Mass.: MIT Press, 1992).

Dupré, John, *The Disorder of Things* (Cambridge, Mass.: Harvard University Press, 1993).

Flew, Antony, 'Locke and the Problem of Personal Identity', *Philosophy*, xxvi (1951) 53–68.

Flew, Antony, *The Logic of Mortality* (Oxford: Blackwell, 1987).

Fodor, J.A., 'Special Sciences', *Synthese*, 28 (1974) 97–115.

Frankfurt, Harry G., 'Alternate Possibilities and Moral Responsibility', *Journal of Philosophy*, lxvi (1969) 829–39.

Frankfurt, Harry G., 'Freedom of the Will and the Concept of a Person', *Journal of Philosophy*, lxviii (1971) 5–20.

Gaita, Raimond, *Good and Evil* (London: Macmillan Press – now Palgrave, 1991).

Glover, Jonathan (ed.), *The Philosophy of Mind* (Oxford University Press, 1976).

Guttenplan, Samuel (ed.), *A Companion to the Philosophy of Mind* (Oxford: Blackwell, 1994).

Hacker, P.M.S., *Wittgenstein* (London: Phoenix, 1997).

Haldane, John, 'Understanding Folk', *Proceedings of the Aristotelian Society*, Supplementary Volume LXII (1988) 223–54.

Hampshire, Stuart, 'The Analogy of Feeling', *Mind*, 71 (1952) 1–12.

Hampshire, Stuart, 'Feeling and Expression', in Glover (ed.), *The Philosophy of Mind* (1976).

Hanfling, Oswald, *Wittgenstein's Later Philosophy* (London: Macmillan Press – now Palgrave, 1989).

Heidegger, Martin, *Being and Time*, trans. John Macquarrie and Edward Robinson (New York: Harper and Row, 1962).

Hertzberg Lars, 'Blame and Causality', *Mind*, 84 (1975) 500–15.

Honderich, Ted, *How Free Are You?* (Oxford University Press, 1993).

Hume, David, *A Treatise of Human Nature* (1739), Book I ed. D.G.C. Macnabb (Glasgow: Collins, 1962).

Jackson, Frank and Pettit, Philip, 'Causation in the Philosophy of Mind', *Philosophy and Phenomenological Research*, 59 (1989–90) 195–214.

Kenny, Anthony, *Descartes: a Study of his Philosophy* (New York: Random House, 1968).

Kenny, Anthony, *The Metaphysics of Mind* (Oxford University Press, 1989).

Kerr, Fergus, *Theology After Wittgenstein* (Oxford: Blackwell, 1986).

Kim, Jaegwon, 'Epiphenomenalism and Supervenient Causation', in Rosenthal (ed.), *The Nature of Mind* (1991).

Kim, Jaegwon, *Supervenience and Mind* (Cambridge University Press, 1993).

Kim, Jaegwon, *Philosophy of Mind* (Oxford: Westview Press, 1996).

Kim, Jaegwon, 'Supervenience', in Guttenplan (ed.) *A Companion to the Philosophy of Mind* (1994).

Lewis, David, 'Mad Pain and Martian Pain', in Rosenthal (ed.) *The Nature of Mind* (1991).

Lewis, David, 'Lewis David: Reduction of Mind', in Guttenplan (ed.) *A Companion to the Philosophy of Mind* (1994).

Locke, John, *An Essay Concerning Human Understanding* (1690), ed A.D. Woozley (Glasgow: Collins, 1964).

Long, D.C., 'The Philosophical Concept of the Human Body', *Philosophical Review*, 73 (1964) 321–37.

Lorimer, David, *Survival? Body, Mind and Death in the Light of Psychic Experience* (London: Routledge & Kegan Paul, 1984).

Lowe, E.J., 'The Causal Autonomy of the Mental', *Mind*, 102 (1993) 629–44.

Lycan, G. (ed.), *Mind and Cognition: a Reader* (Oxford: Blackwell, 1990).

Malcolm, Norman, 'Knowledge of Other Minds', *Journal of Philosophy*, 55 (1958), 969–78.

Malcolm, Norman, 'Scientific Materialism and the Identity Theory', *Dialogue*, 3 (1964) 116–19.

Malcolm, Norman, *Problems of Mind* (London: Allen & Unwin, 1971).

McDonald, C., *Mind–Body Identity Theories* (London: Routledge & Kegan Paul, 1989).

McGinn, Marie, *Wittgenstein and the Philosophical Investigations* (London: Routledge, 1997).

MacIntyre, A.C., 'Determinism', *Mind*, lxvi (1957) 28–41.

Mill, J.S., *An Examination of Sir William Hamilton's Philosophy*, 6th edn (London, 1889).

Mulhall, Stephen, *Heidegger and Being and Time* (London: Routledge, 1996).

Nowell-Smith, P.H., 'Freewill and Moral Responsibility', *Mind*, lvii (1948) 45–61.

Parfit, Derek, 'Personal Identity', *Philosophical Review*, 80 (1971) 3–27.

Parfit, Derek, *Reasons and Persons* (Oxford: Clarendon Press, 1984).

Perry, John, *A Dialogue on Personal Identity and Immortality* (Indianapolis: Hackett, 1978).

Perry, John (ed.), *Personal Identity* (Berkeley and Los Angeles: University of California Press, 1975).

Pettit, Phillip, 'A Definition of Physicalism', *Analysis*, 53 (4) (1993) 213–23.

Place, U.T., 'Is Consciousness a Brain Process?', *British Journal of Psychology*, 47 (1956) 44–50.

Putnam, Hilary, 'The "Meaning" of Meaning', in his *Mind, Languages and Reality: Philosophical Papers*, Vol. 2 (Cambridge University Press, 1975).

Rosenthal, David M. (ed.), *The Nature of Mind* (Oxford University Press, 1991).

Quinton, Antony, 'The Soul', *The Journal of Philosophy*, lix (1962) 363–409.

Ryle, Gilbert, *The Concept of Mind* (Harmondsworth: Penguin, 1949).

Ryle, Gilbert, 'The World of Science and the Everyday World', in Ryle, *Dilemmas* (Cambridge University Press, 1966).

Sacks, Oliver, *An Anthropologist on Mars* (London: Picador, 1995).

Searle, John, *Minds, Brains and Science* (Harmondsworth: Penguin, 1984).

Searle, John, 'Is the Brain's Mind a Computer Program?', *Scientific American*, (January 1990) 20–5.

Searle, John, 'Searle, John R.', in Guttenplan (ed.), *A Companion to the Philosophy of Mind* (1994).

Sharpe, R.A., 'The Very Idea of a Folk Psychology', *Inquiry*, 30 (1987) 381–93.

Singer, Peter, *Animal Liberation* (New York: Avon, 1978).

Smart, J.J.C., 'Sensations and Brain Processes', *Philosophical Review*, 68 (1959), 141–56.

Smith, Peter and Jones, O.R., *The Philosophy of Mind: an Introduction* (Cambridge University Press, 1986).

Squires, Roger, 'On One's Mind', *Philosophical Quarterly*, 20 (1970) 347–56.

Squires, Roger, 'Zombies v Materialists', *Proceedings of the Aristotelian Society*, Supplementary Volume xlviii (1974) 153–63.

Stevenson, Ian, *Twenty Cases Suggestive of Reincarnation* (Charlottesville: University Press of Virginia, 1974).

Strawson, P.F., 'Persons', in Strawson, *Individuals* (London: Methuen, 1959).

Strawson, P.F., 'Freedom and Resentment', *Proceedings of the British Academy*, xlviii (1962) 1–25.

Swinburne, Richard, *The Evolution of the Soul* (Oxford University Press, 1986).

Taylor, Charles, *Sources of the Self* (Cambridge University Press, 1989).

Tilghman, Ben, *Wittgenstein, Ethics and Aesthetics: the View From Eternity* (Basingstoke: Macmillan – now Palgrave, 1991).

Turing, A.M., 'Computing Machinery and Intelligence', *Mind*, 59 (1950) 433–60.

Tye, Michael, 'Naturalism and the Mental', *Mind*, 101 (1992) 421–41.

Watson, Gary (ed.), *Free Will* (Oxford University Press, 1982).

Watson, Gary, 'Responsibility and the Limits of Evil: Variations on a Strawsonian Theme', in Ferdinand Schoeman (ed.), *Responsibility, Character and the Emotions* (Cambridge University Press, 1987).

Watson, J.B. and McDougall, W., *The Battle of Behaviourism* (Kegan Paul, 1928).

Wilkes, K.V., 'Pragmatics in Science and Theory in Common Sense', *Inquiry*, 27 (1984) 339–61.

Williams, Bernard, *Problems of the Self* (Cambridge University Press, 1973).

Williams, Bernard, *Descartes: the Project of Pure Enquiry* (Harmondsworth: Penguin, 1978).

Winch, Peter, "Eine Einstellung Zur Seele", in Winch, *Trying to Make Sense* (Oxford: Blackwell, 1987).

Wittgenstein, Ludwig, *The Blue and Brown Books* (Oxford: Basil Blackwell, 1958).

Wittgenstein, Ludwig, *Philosophical Investigations*, eds G.E.M. Anscombe, G.H. von Wright and R. Rhees, trans G.E.M. Anscombe (Oxford: Blackwell, 1968).

Wittgenstein, Ludwig, *Zettel*, eds G.E.M. Anscombe and G.H. von Wright, trans. G.E.M. Anscombe (Oxford: Blackwell, 1967).

Wittgenstein, Ludwig, *On Certainty*, eds G.E.M. Anscombe and G.H. von Wright, trans. Denis Paul and G.E.M. Anscombe (Oxford: Blackwell, 1969).

Wittgenstein, Ludwig, 'Cause and Effect: Intuitive Awareness', ed. Rush Rhees, trans. Peter Winch, *Philosophia*, 6 (1976) 409–25.

Wolf, Susan, *Freedom Within Reason* (Oxford University Press, 1990).

Index